DEVON & CORNWALL

Edited by Simon Harwin

First published in Great Britain in 2002 by
YOUNG WRITERS
Remus House,
Coltsfoot Drive,
Peterborough, PE2 9JX
Telephone (01733) 890066

All Rights Reserved

Copyright Contributors 2002

HB ISBN 0 75434 006 6
SB ISBN 0 75434 007 4

FOREWORD

This year, Young Writers proudly presents a showcase of the best short stories and creative writing from today's up-and-coming writers.

We set the challenge of writing for one of our four themes - 'General Short Stories', 'Ghost Stories', 'Tales With A Twist' and 'A Day In The Life Of . . .'. The effort and imagination expressed by each individual writer was more than impressive and made selecting entries an enjoyable, yet demanding, task.

Write On! Devon & Cornwall is a collection that we feel you are sure to enjoy - featuring the very best young authors of the future. Their hard work and enthusiasm clearly shines within these pages, highlighting the achievement each story represents.

We hope you are as pleased with the final selection as we are and that you will continue to enjoy this special collection for many years to come.

CONTENTS

Bridestowe Primary School, Devon
- Ruth Hatton — 1

Charlestown CP School, Cornwall
- Peter Wheeler — 2
- Adam Smith — 3
- Alison Hodkin — 4
- Paige Trethewey — 6
- Emma Harris — 7
- Cameron Kelly — 8
- Holly Roberts — 9
- Rosanna Blatchford — 10
- Ross Belcher — 11
- Amy Sharma Bassie — 12
- Caroline Harvey — 13
- Sam Crocker — 14
- Elsie Richardson — 15
- Abby Bate — 16
- Rhiannon Leopold — 17

Crowan Primary School, Cornwall
- Joe Pawluk — 18
- Gemma Smith — 19
- Josh Bates — 20
- Lana Harris — 21
- Jessy Kennely — 22
- Jessica Fairlie — 23
- Bethany Robinson — 24
- Andrew Streatfield — 25
- Georgina Lloyd — 26
- Jack Edwards — 27
- Raglan Thompson — 28
- Luke Hilliard — 29
- Mark Spalding-Jenkin — 30

John Stocker Middle School, Devon

Danika Cosway-Richardson	31
Rebecca Cohead	32
Jodie Brush	34
James Tylisczuk	35
Karen Elson	36
Lucy Roke	38
Sarah Chakmakchi	39
Rebecca Webb	40
Robert Browning	41
Eleanor Spencer	42
Bethany Connett	43
Jasmine Davey	44
Mark Foster	45

Manor House School, Devon

Emily Shields	46
Georgina Hunt	47
Harriet Carr	48
Katya Moore	49
Sam Kallaway	50
Harry Edmanson	51
Christopher Pomeroy	52
Alex Macadam	53
James Welch-Thornton	54
Holly Ford	55
Harry Lawrence	56
Oliver Persey	57
Isobel Caton Harrison	58
Thomas Auckland	59
Tom Vanstone	60
Cressida Auckland	61
Matthew Hutchings	62
Jocelyn Trayler-Clarke	63
Ben Matthews	64
Kate Edwards	65
Camilla Fisher Crouch	66
Freddie Galley	67

Kit Kelsey	68
Gaby Fielding	69
Kirstin Maclean	70
Demelza Trezise	71
Beth Luxton	72
Eddie Morrison	73
William Mostyn	74
Charlie Pepworth	75
Emma Hurford	76
Calista Trayler-Clarke	77
Georgia Wells	78
Edward Parr	79
Amelia Figgins	80
James Wells	81
Rebecca Taylor	82
Timothy Hughes	83
Annie Parr	84
Annabel Lumley	85

Plympton St Maurice Primary School, Devon

Michael Arries	86
Richard Carne	87
Nesha Clemens	88
Isabelle Fitzgerald	89
Timothy Hanrahan	90
Joshua Howarth	91
Matthew Keane	92
Kieran Painter	93
David Pryke	94
Holly Rixon	95
Carl Smith	96
Morwenna Summerhill	97
Dane Willcocks	98
Jessica Willcocks	99
Joanna Lewis	100
Chris Tomlinson	101
Latesha Claffey	102
Bradley Ball	103

Charlotte Vosper	104
Bradley Warren	1005
Leah Cragg	106
Andrew Endean	107
Thomas Brown	108
Harry Sherwin	109
Emily Pope	110
Thomas Downs	111
Joshua Egan	112
Alex Neville	113
Shawn Norton	114
Jordan Powlesland	115

Werrington Primary School, Cornwall

Craig Hunkin	116
Bob Carr	117
Jack Basford	118
Alice Warring	119
Abigail Williams	120
Ben Jenkin	121

West Hill Primary School, Devon

Michael Hall	122
Alistair Slade	123
Aimée Snell	124
Michael Rose	125
April Down	126
Elinor Puttick	127
Billy Hesmondhalgh	128
Katie Light	129
Kathryn Rowles	130
Samuel Bowker	131
Melissa Crombie	132
Peter Cowan	133
Camilla Russell	134
Rebecca James	135
Amelia Colwill	136

Mercedes Pemberton-Finch	137
Joseph Tomlins	138

Whitstone Primary School, Devon

Louise Adamson	139
Ben Roberts & Thomas Gerry	140
Nicholas Coleing	141
Izzy Hamilton	142
Stacey Bluett	143
Claire Bluett & Samantha Collins	144
Stephen Martin	145

The Stories

A Day In The Life Of Henry VIII, 1520

I am fed up with that measly King Francis of France claiming he is better than me. I'm going to show him that I'm Europe's top dog; that I'm the best king there is!

I have held a boasting tournament. I named it, 'The Field Of The Cloth Of Gold.' I showed off my magnificent palace, my huge army and my wonderful English food. There were sports of all kinds. You should have seen Francis' face when an English knight beat him at jousting! I was extremely pleased because I beat him in the wrestling, even though he cheated. The archery was good fun too, but I swear the bullseye Francis hit was a fluke.

Every night, I threw a brilliant party. When we departed, I told Francis I was sorry he had to go, but in truth, I couldn't wait to see the slimy back of him leave.

As soon as we parted, I went and started plotting with Charles V of the Holy Roman Empire. I expect he has forgotten about my assault ages ago, he seems to have forgiven me for turning on him after we beat the French.

Ruth Hatton (11)
Bridestowe Primary School, Devon

A Day In The Life Of A Reticulated Python

Back in time, how fantastic I felt! We always have been fascinated by pythons and here I am as one. I am a reticulated python, the longest snake in the world. I will grow to ten metres long.

One day, I was slithering through the South American rainforest looking for my tea, when I came across a rodent. I lay in wait, then crept up and wrapped myself around its body in my powerful coils until it suffocated, as I am not a poisonous snake, then I swallowed it whole. After my snack, I slithered around the rainforest for a little while, when I found that my skin was coming off. As a young snake, my skin comes off seven or more times a year, because my skin gets worn and damaged, and to let me grow. So off came my old skin and my new one was bigger, it felt great.

I felt tired after I had shed my skin and had my snack, so I found somewhere to sleep, somewhere that I would blend into the background of the rainforest. After my sleep, I will look for a larger meal.

Peter Wheeler (9)
Charlestown CP School, Cornwall

A Day In The Life Of Jimmy Floyd Hasselbaink

I woke up in a warm, comfy double bed, hungry and ready for breakfast. It was a beautiful, sunny day outside. Eating my Sporties, I jumped into the nice, warm shower. I stepped out of the sparkling clean shower and started to rub myself with a blue fluffy towel. I put on my navy blue suit with matching tie. There was a pair of black, gleaming shoes in the corner of my room, which I put on. I walked down the stairs with great pride.

I stepped outside and went for a spin in my new Ferrari convertible. I came back to hear a great big crowd of fans shouting. I signed a few autographs and then I climbed onto the bus. We drove off to Stamford Bridge.

We got changed and went out onto the green, grassed football pitch, for a bit of training before the match and then we went in the changing room to hear the tactics.

We marched out onto the pitch, the referee blew his whistle, the ball got passed to me. I struck it so hard that the ball flew past Barthez into the top corner. It was 1-0 and it stayed like that, we were the champions.

We drove off back to the hotel for tea. I walked to my room and fell asleep. The next morning, I woke up and I was just plain, old Adam Smith.

Adam Smith (9)
Charlestown CP School, Cornwall

A Day In The Life Of Bournville (My Dog)

Click! The old, rusty key turned in its stiff lock. Short and jolly as ever, my owner stumbled into my conservatory. Slowly and steadily I emerged from the blankets and plodded to the open door. Outside it was dark and the warm breeze whipped my thick brown fur as I strolled across the wet, green grass. Then my eyes lit up dangerously. I went tearing through the bushes and leapt over the lowest part of the wall, with great difficulty.

Nearly half a mile away from home, I spun around. There wasn't anyone there. My heart sank 10,000 feet. Instantly I threw my nose the ground, sniffing for all I was worth. After a while I bumped into something big and skinny. Startled and partly hopeful I looked up. A tall, grim-looking boxer was looking down at me with disgust and anger. 'Who are you?' he sneered.
'B-B-Bournville,' I murmured.
'Well, get out of here! This area is mine!' the boxer barked.
I went!

I was getting hungry, so depending on my nose, I started to try and find some food. It didn't take me long to find a little butchers, right in the middle of nowhere. Crawling noiselessly towards my target, I snatched a huge, mouth-watering slice of pork. Suddenly a door crashed open on my right. A fat, bald man stood there, a mop in one hand and a heart-stopping piece of beef in the other. Eyes popping, the man lunged at me. I went ploughing through bushes and dodging trees with the man slowing down every second.

I sat panting under a large beech tree, then the boxer emerged from behind some tall, beautiful bushes. I was on my feet in half a second. He started to circle. In a voice that was deep and dark, he started to speak, 'You, with your smart collar, why do you want to live with humans? They're dumb,' he sneered. Before I knew what I was doing, I had pounced. Struggling and yelling with pain, he dragged his paw away from my mouth and limped away.

Off I went back home. It was dark when I got home, there were no lights on. I barked and barked. Like a bolt of lightning, the door flew open and there stood my owner. When she saw me, she flung her arms around me and took me upstairs and we snuggled down together. My day of being Bournville the dog was over.

Alison Hodkin (8)
Charlestown CP School, Cornwall

A Day In The Life Of A Beach Dog

Scavenging in the garbage-littered beach, with bones pushing out from beneath my skin, I join the squabble over a pure white bone with a few shreds of meat still clinging onto it.

Eventually, I manage to tear it away from their starving mouths and hurtle away with it. I settle down in the thick, green grass to chew the bone and mix it with my saliva to produce a tasty gravy. My stomach churns contentedly. I doze in the hot sun, hoping to fall into a peaceful sleep, to sleep off my meal.

I awake in the late afternoon. My stomach is rumbling badly. I raise myself to go in search of food. I decide to take a long stroll, all the way down to the Beach Club Restaurant. People shall surely be sitting outside on a hot afternoon like this. The pads of my feet tingle as I slink across the scorched dirt.

I creep around the back of the grey, crumbly walls and enter the tourist eating grounds. There are plenty of tourists dining, as I expected. I raise myself up onto two legs, making sure everyone can see me. I whine, pleadingly, and it works! Someone throws a piece of fresh, bloody meat to me. I gobble it up quickly and licking my lips, I go to lie down in the shade of the palm trees.

But just as I reach them . . . *crack!* A loud boom filled the air. Crack, crack, crack! A few shots sounded, this time closer. A panic breaks out. Dogs scramble into the leaf-covered bushes. I follow, there seems no other option. I realise dogs are being shot.

The hunter looks in my direction and settles his black, beady eyes on me. I only feel swirling and whirling, I can't think, I can't move. But there I am, standing, a human once again.

Paige Trethewey (8)
Charlestown CP School, Cornwall

A Day In The Life Of A Bird

Assembling my beautiful wings, I swooped out into the big, wide world. A little mouse nibbled gingerly on a bright yellow piece of corn. I plummeted down like water gushing from the drainpipe. Silently though, like a swan, I snatched like a robber. In a frenzied dance, I flew back to my nest like rush hour at 8 o'clock in the morning. Snuggled up were my young, like some child's crushed up uniform on a Friday. Little by little, I shared out the food. I felt happy.

Look at my new work of art. I've made it from crooked twigs, moss and leaves. Shoving closely together, my young and I relaxed in our bright, healthy, huge tree. We fell asleep.

Twittering woke me up. Flying off once again to catch food, the weather was terrible, pouring giant tears. Fortunately the worms came up. I collected twenty worms and up I went like an aeroplane taking off.

I fed my young, the delight on their faces was unbelievable. One shivered like lapping, smooth waves. I wrapped my wings around their cold bodies and they heated up like an oven. We huddled our little bodies together and dozed off.

Waking up to the boiling hot sunshine blazing through the trees, friends twittered and sang as I watched a hummingbird flutter off into the mouth of an oak tree.

Emma Harris (9)
Charlestown CP School, Cornwall

A Day In The Life Of Kylie Minogue

Stepping into my luxurious jacuzzi, I sighed with pleasure. Bubbles the colours of the rainbow floated around me as I soaked my old bones, but the relaxation didn't last. I got out of the jacuzzi and dried myself in my dressing room. It had a huge plaque saying, *The One And Only Kylie Minogue.*

The make-up artist had unpacked her tools and indicated for me to sit. I plonked my bottom down on a really comfy seat. She put a gown on me so she didn't spill anything on my clothes. She slapped the pancake stage make-up on nice and thick, to fill in the cracks, and enough lip gloss so that if I kissed you, I'd slide right off!

The hairdresser killed every bug and fly in the area with the amount of hairspray she used to glue my hair in place. Only a hurricane could move it.

Here we go again, more photographs of me crammed into another corset mini dress. I know it's for my new album cover, but I'll go mad if the photographer asks me to stick my bottom out again.

I'm so tired, and there's still a new single to record before the end of the day. Then there's another champagne party to attend - it's tough being a superstar!

Cameron Kelly (9)
Charlestown CP School, Cornwall

A DAY IN THE LIFE OF A DOLPHIN TRAINER

Putting the dead, goggle-eyed fish in the silver bucket, I thought how rewarding it will be to feed my wide-eyed dolphin friends. In what seemed like no time, I began to walk to the water's edge where Orlando, Starbuck and Dolly were playing. Out of my eye, I saw the two new baby, smily dolphins, with the other trainers.

After one hour of playing fantastic games, feeding them their favourite fish, it's now time to get ready for an excellent morning show, watching all the people running or walking into the large, hot stadium that is now full.

Starting the performance was Becky, in her pink wetsuit. Quite quickly, it was my lovely time of swimming with the dolphins. Diving with straight legs into the salt water, I'm swimming now with all these people watching me. I'm trying my very best. Spinning around, holding the dolphins' flippers, I felt dizzy. I jumped on the platform and chased a seagull and fell in the cold pool. Climbing back on the slippery platform, I got stinky fish and fed them to my lovely dolphins.

Going backstage into the white lighthouse, I started to speak to Liz.
I said, 'What time is the next great show?'
'12:15,' she shouted.

I squeezed the water out of my shiny, long hair and started to play with my lovely dolphin friends. 'Time is going very slowly till the next show,' I whispered to my favourite dolphin.

As the best day ever carried on, it got more exciting as the hours went by. I just hope that I can have another exciting experience another day in my happy life.

Holly Roberts (9)
Charlestown CP School, Cornwall

A Day In The Life Of Phi Phi

So here I am. What is that delicious smell? I shall investigate. Mmmm, chicken. That was a tasty meal. Oh no, there's an enormous giant coming after me, it's shouting my name. The giant is picking me up, up, up, but squeezing me at the same time.

I see how high we are, it is frightening. We are obviously going up the creaky, old stairs. The big, noisy giant places me on a high bed. The giant pushes me off the scary bed. I miaowed as loud as I could.

I ran down the wooden stairs. A lady picked me up, but she didn't squeeze me. The lady was neat and tidy, she gently placed me safely on a comfy blanket. I started to lick myself. It feels strange, I'm warm and cosy, I shall have a happy dream in the sun as it reflects in the untidy front room.

I dreamt that I was floating on a cloud bed. Suddenly, I felt some fingers squashing me. I woke up cold, someone was pulling me by my tail into a very thorny bush.

Rosanna Blatchford (8)
Charlestown CP School, Cornwall

A Day In The Life Of An Acrobat

I go to bed and quickly go to sleep. I dream about me being an acrobat for a day.

In the morning, I was amazed, I found myself in a colourful caravan with my circus clothes hanging on the wall. I hear a banging sound outside, then I notice my dream has come true!

I look outside, to my amazement the tent had been put up. 'Whoo! I've never, ever seen a tent as big as that before! The circus is coming to town!'
Bill shouted, 'Come over here.' Bill explained he was the ringmaster. 'Quick, get on stage,' Bill said hurriedly.

I climbed up the rope to the trapeze and started swinging. I tried to do the triple, but I couldn't. I fell and fell. Suddenly, I hit the bar at the bottom and fainted. I was alright. I climbed up the rope to the trapeze and started swinging until I was high enough to let go and do the triple, until I got it right. Later, in front of all the crowd, I did the triple perfectly!

I went to my caravan and fell asleep, and when I woke up, I was in my own little bed. It was all a dream.

Ross Belcher (8)
Charlestown CP School, Cornwall

A Day In The Life Of A Pig

So here I am as a pig, no one to tell me what to do all the time. Then suddenly, someone or something jumped out of nowhere. The sudden thing threw an orange thing at me. I grunted and sniffed it. It smelt like something familiar. I swallowed it in a big gulp. The thing threw more and more. Swallowing them as fast as I could, I was thinking, what am I eating?

A slight sound hit my ears at once. A bang and a crunch. Something was behind me. I spun around and there behind me was the fattest pig ever. I didn't dare turn around at all. I grunted and grunted again. I was looking at him in despair. 'Who are you? What are you doing in my place?'
The big pig opened his large mouth and shouted, 'You're in my place, you twit!'

I got to the wall. 'Aaahhhhh!' In other words, 'Grunnnnnnt!' The thing which had thrown something at me came running over again. It opened the gate as I backed out. Suddenly, my two back legs fell down a hole. I just wish I had never wanted to be a pig. It's terrible being a pig, just terrible!

Suddenly, I turned back to myself. I felt sick, I had eaten orange skin.

Amy Sharma Bassie (9)
Charlestown CP School, Cornwall

A DAY IN THE LIFE OF A DOCTOR

Walking down the corridor, breathing in the clean air of the brand new hospital, I felt like a real doctor. A nurse was calling my name, 'Dr Harvey.'

Running quickly down the corridor, I saw a patient was waiting in the operating theatre for me. Seeing the patient crying, needing my help, I said to my nurses, 'This won't be easy. Give me my pincers.'
'Dr Harvey, I will sort you out,' answered Sarah.
'She's got gallstones,' I shouted.

After finishing the operation, it was time for our mouth-watering lunch. 'It's been hard work,' I sighed. They all agreed. Before I had finished my lunch, I heard the loud speaker's voice,
'Dr Harvey, please come to the reception area.'
'Must dash!' I cried.

A little girl was being pushed on a trolley through the doors by the ambulance men. She had been in a car crash. 'We will have to put your leg in a plaster,' I said, as I pushed her into the operating theatre.

My tummy started to rumble and I realised it was going to be a long wait until my tea.

I do want to be a doctor when I grow up.

Caroline Harvey (8)
Charlestown CP School, Cornwall

A Day In The Life Of A Tortoise

So, I'm a tortoise. How did this happen? I don't know, but I suppose I should find my breakfast. I'll try this furry, green plant. Yuk! Mint! I detest mint, but that yellowy-green one must be delicious, because all the other tortoises are eating it.

Plodding around with this heavy shell on my back feels very odd, although I don't need to find shelter because I can just plop my head and legs in my shell.

I'm back on track looking for a friend to talk to, when I stumble over a large rock and find myself on my shell. I'm trying to get back onto my chubby legs, when I see a giant bird with a sharp beak staring at me, like I'm its dinner. I yell, 'Help! Help!' and suddenly there is a rustle from the undergrowth and out charges a heavily armoured tortoise. He is trying to tip me over, but I can see the bird dribbling. My new friend pushes me over at last and we both run as fast as we can for cover.

After all we have been through, we decide to go on a journey to find a safer home. We will start at dawn.

Sam Crocker (9)
Charlestown CP School, Cornwall

A Day In The Life Of A Rabbit

Suddenly, I was free in the fresh, green field, as morning arrived on top of the headland cliff. Staring into the fabulous world ahead, I hopped about a bit, then I ran down a big green hill. At the bottom, I dug a little hole and I scurried inside. I was a little nervous about people running around on the lush field.

Clomp, stamp, noisy feet clambering around me. Peering faces looking down at me. There I sat, wondering when the big feet and pink faces would ever leave me alone, nervously nibbling the juicy, green grass.

Down I fell, deep to the bottom of my burrow. It was all dark and gloomy and not very pleasant at all, I don't know how the other rabbits could live down a horrible place like this. It's where all the slimy slugs and filthy worms live, not rabbits.

I jumped out of the disgusting place and my eyes nearly went blind because of the scorching sunlight. I blinked my eyes to get used to the sun, then hopped to the nearest shady tree.

Elsie Richardson (9)
Charlestown CP School, Cornwall

A Day In The Life Of An Elephant

I saw muddy, runny water glazing in the sun. A splash of muddy water hit my long trunk and it ran down, like a colony of ants. I wallow in mud that runs thick, like a river of porridge.

As the day progresses, the temperature rises, I have to flap my ears frantically in order to keep myself cool.

I slowly advance into the depths of the savage jungle with my herd. As we get more into the jungle, I get pricked by brambles and stroked by leaves. I have to face fierce animals like lions, tigers and hyenas. There were ugly rats and mice scuttling around the dirty floor. I saw monkeys swing from tree to tree at night and in the morning.

The evil tigers, lions and hyenas pounce on our backs every day and night. Every day, the hyenas chase the rats and mice up the trees, round the bushes and through the leaves.

I plod over the hard rocks, making sure I don't topple over on my huge side as we pass the little river. Then suddenly . . . *crash, smash, bang, wallop!* I fall.

Abby Bate (8)
Charlestown CP School, Cornwall

A Day In The Life Of Amy Bassie

I woke up to Amy's sisters' electric toothbrushes. I'll call them my sisters, for today anyway. So I'd better make the most of this experience.

I put on my clothes and then I had my breakfast. After that, I put on my boots and a raincoat and set off to call for my friends. Why on earth do I keep calling everything mine, when they are not mine, they are Amy's?

I probably should tell you why I chose to be my friend, Amy Bassie, for this, 'a day in the life of someone.' It's because Amy's got everyone as her friend and she lives in a static caravan, while her dad builds the house, and she gets cool clothes and ever since I moved into Charlestown school, I've always wanted to be Amy Bassie. So here I am as who I wanted to be. Amy Bassie, the most popular girl in our entire class.

I am very grateful for this opportunity, and now you can meet Amy's friends. Their names are Becky, Ben, Jason, Ricky, Amy, Ben, oh my - another Ben, another Amy. I think I'm going to forget who I am. So, that's the way I'd like to be.

Rhiannon Leopold (8)
Charlestown CP School, Cornwall

A Day In The Life Of A Cat

Yum! This is nice. Chicken and liver, my favourite breakfast. I think it's time for bed now, up the stairs to my owner. My loving owner strokes me. I purr as loud as I can to show him my affection. Oh no, he has to go to work. Oh well, must be time to go to sleep.

I must have slept till four o'clock. I jump off the bed and clamber down the stairs to the kitchen, to wait for my tea. I drink some water to pass the time. At last, my owner comes home and I miaow to get my tea early. This time, I have duck in jelly, one of my other favourites.

A few hours later, I settle down on my owner's lap and watch some telly with him. When he goes to bed, he puts me in the kitchen, where I settle down for the night.

Joe Pawluk (10)
Crowan Primary School, Cornwall

WHAT I SAW

I came up my street. Everything looked pretty much as it usually did. However, as I opened my front door, I couldn't believe what I saw. To my horror, the glasses were smashed. I ran to the living room, where I saw the sofas ripped. I yelped for Mum, but no answer came back. I quickly rushed to Mum's room where I saw a black cloak clinging to a hanger, and it hit me.

I dragged myself to the calendar next to Mum's bed. On April 1st it was April Fool's Day, which came very quickly, because as long as I can remember it was only March 21st. But anyway, people often called me Forgetful Frankie and you will be surprised how time goes by.

Was this a joke? It certainly wasn't a joke to me. To be honest, I was pretty freaked out.

Suddenly, I looked in the mirror to find a spooky clown. I jumped out of my skin. I looked him up and down. His green dungarees and stupid yellow shoes reminded me of something. Mum! Mum had big feet and as I built up my courage, I jumped up and pulled of the mask. It was Mum, looking cross, but kind of laughing.
'Happy Fool's Day, Frankie,' she said.
'What?' I shrieked.
'I was going to surprise you!'
'By scaring me? It wasn't funny.'
She hugged me and said sorry.

Next time when it's April Fool's Day, don't get freaked out. After all, people who play pranks are really fools!

Gemma Smith (10)
Crowan Primary School, Cornwall

A DAY IN THE LIFE OF AN ANT

I was dashing across the huge, concrete path, heading straight for the colony on the other side, when I heard an ear-splitting crash. Once, twice, three times and getting louder and closer by the minute!

Suddenly, a gigantic foot slammed past me, the impact knocking me back all the way to the side of the path. It was that dreadful boy again, that was the third time this week! Everyone at the colony would really be wondering where I was! Oh well, back to square one again! So I took my chances and started to dash across the huge concrete path . . .

Josh Bates (11)
Crowan Primary School, Cornwall

A Day In The Life Of A Spider

I woke up this morning, only to find a blazing light dazzling my eyesight. It was the morning dew sticking to my web. A buzzing noise was coming closer and closer, it came from the other side of my web. It was a most scrumptious house fly, dropping every second nearer to me. I could just taste the fly.

Suddenly, my web was disturbed by a shake. I turned my head, only to find it destroyed by a girl, a girl who was so bored she had dismantled part of it by using a long, brown, fat stick.

The girl caught a glimpse of me and started screaming continuously, like a screeching car going extremely fast. I quickly slid down the grass stalk and gradually escaped.

There was that noise again. I looked up and saw the fly happily flying away to safety. I made a new web where no one could get near, or see me anymore.

A few weeks later, I saw that same fly zoom past. I hid where I could not be seen. Finally, I caught the fly. It was mine, at last!

Lana Harris (11)
Crowan Primary School, Cornwall

A Day In The Life Of Winnie The Pooh

What was that? The door? I can't stand up! Oh well, I've got honey. Do you want some? *Tough!* Honey, I must have more honey, it's all gooey and sticky and deliciously sweet. It wouldn't be possible to live without honey! Honey, honey, honey, it's a rich bear's world!

Yikes, Tigger's coming, run! But I can't, I just can't leave all my sweet honey! *Crash! Bang!* My honey, my beautiful honey. It's gone, all gone!

Jessy Kennely (11)
Crowan Primary School, Cornwall

A Day In The Life Of My Hamster

8am   Wake up, stretch legs, climb out of bed. Yawn, yawn, very tired!
8:30   Nibble, nibble, tasty raspberry hamster food. My favourite!
10:00   Slurrpp, so refreshing. Delicious water!
10:30   Climb into bed, get nice and comfy in fluffy bed.
11:00   Fall asleep. Very cosy!
12 noon Fast asleep. Extremely comfortable!
2:00   Wake up. Stroll out of bed.
2:15   Go to the toilet. Feel much better.
3:00   Jess put me in my ball to run around for two whole hours. So exhausting!
5:00   Climb into cage. Go to bed.
8:00   Fast asleep.

8am   Wake up . . .

Jessica Fairlie (10)
Crowan Primary School, Cornwall

A Day In The Life Of A Cat

My paws are wet and cold, ice-cold. My tummy is rumbling like a small toy train. I hear a rustling sound in the bush. I creep up to it and see a fat, juicy rat. Pouncing on it, I gobble it up. Delicious.

Suddenly, from around the corner comes a tall black dog, it starts to chase me, so I run as fast as I can, around the corner and up the wall, where the dog can't find me.

I see the window of my house is open, so I jump in and run straight to my favourite room, the lounge, and sit in front of the warm, cosy fire and fall asleep. Safe at last.

Bethany Robinson (10)
Crowan Primary School, Cornwall

A Day In The Life Of A Leopard

I woke up this morning to the delight of an antelope nearby. Yum! I crouched in the tall grass, padded to an area where I could see it clearly, then pounced. I caught it by surprise, but it still put up a good fight. I slowly ate it, bite by bite, then . . . *growl.*

I leapt into the grass - hyenas! I fought to save my breakfast, but when I scared one hyena away, three more came. I was overwhelmed, so I leaped into a tree, then I saw the owner of this territory coming . . . a lion! I ran as fast as I could, but it kept up as if I as still. Then it leapt onto me . . . *thud!*

Andrew Streatfield (10)
Crowan Primary School, Cornwall

A Day In The Life Of Piglet

I'm getting so bored up here. I'm just desperate to get off this shelf. I'll pull and I'll push and I'll . . . ahhhh! OK, I got what I wanted. I'm down on the floor, so now I can be like everybody else. I'm running around quickly now, looking for something to do or see. Oh no, the cat, it's after me. It's pouncing at me. I run faster and faster. I'm puffed out. I climb up onto the dresser. I'm safe. And then comes another danger, a buzzy bee. Buzzzz, it goes.
'Shut up! Shut up!' I shout.

It's chaos around the house. I keep on tripping over things. The bee must have got tired and given up. I climb hastily up onto the desk and then onto the shelf. I think I'll just stay here. That was a big mistake.

Georgina Lloyd (10)
Crowan Primary School, Cornwall

A DAY IN THE LIFE OF A ROCK

Hi, I am a rock. I don't do anything, other than sit, look and get stepped on! Most people don't think that I've got eyes, *but I have!* And I have feelings, so go away . . .

Jack Edwards (10)
Crowan Primary School, Cornwall

THE LOST WORLD

I was on a gentle stroll in the countryside, when I felt the ground beneath me shake. Suddenly, a giant hole appeared in front of me. A crack went in-between my feet and then it opened up and I fell right down, bouncing from side to side of the deep, dark hole.

Bang! I hit the bottom and looked up to see a light the size of a pea from where I fell. Looking around, I saw a tunnel, so I went over to it and crawled through. When I reached the other side, I couldn't believe what I saw . . . a massive building, five times the size of the Eiffel Tower. I stood up and walked over to the door.

It looked deserted, but after a few minutes, I saw strange animals running around me. I quickly opened the door and ran inside. The creatures circled the building for a while, as I explored the inside. There were steps everywhere. First I went to the top and looked off the balcony. I saw hundreds of other buildings. I had found The Lost Land.

Raglan Thompson (10)
Crowan Primary School, Cornwall

THE CITY OF CHOCOLATE

Billy strolled down the street, staring at his feet, wishing that something would happen. Suddenly, he stepped on a small, glistening stone, ruby red and the size of a tomato. Billy picked it up and stared at it. He rubbed the stone and the words 'Wish, Billy, wish' appeared on it. Billy wished. He wished that the city was made of chocolate, and it worked. The city was made of chocolate. He was standing on a chocolate pavement, there was a chocolate church, a hot chocolate fountain, chocolate grass and even chocolate houses. Everything in the city was chocolate. Billy cheered and then began to eat the creamy brown chocolate, enjoying the taste.

When Billy got home, the first question the was asked was, 'Why is the city made of chocolate?'
'Oh, I wished for it with the tomato thing,' he replied, licking the walls.
'Well, go and find the tomato thing and change it back, because the sun will come out and melt it all into hot chocolate.'
So Billy went back and found the tomato thing and wished back. But the tomato thing did not work, as it had run out of wishes.
'That's a pity, I don't like hot chocolate,' he said.

Luke Hilliard (10)
Crowan Primary School, Cornwall

A Day In The Life Of St George

Into the dark cave I go. 'Where's the dragon?' I ask myself, while jumping over a deep hole filled with bubbling lava.
'Grrrrr,'
'What was that?' said I.

Suddenly the pit of lava overflowed and a red dragon appeared. I ran and ran until I tripped over a stupid rock! The hungry dragon flew over and blew fire at me, so I hid behind my trusty shield with a red cross on it. It flew over again, but this time I was ready. I stuck my sword into the air and the dragon flew into it. It was dead! Or was it?

Mark Spalding-Jenkin (10)
Crowan Primary School, Cornwall

MOUSE GIRL

In a deep, dark wood one sunny day, there was a girl who was picking flowers. A wizard appeared. They had a very terrible fight, then the wizard picked up his wand and turned her into a mouse. The wizard shouted, 'You are going to stay like that for thirteen hours, then you'll realise that you shouldn't be foolish for wanting to be a wizard at only five years old.'
'H-How did you know that?' exclaimed the mouse girl.
'Well, I am a wizard,' sneered the wizard. Then he disappeared into thin air.

An hour passed . . . then ten hours passed . . . the mouse girl was wishing that she had never been so foolish. Then another hour passed and eventually, she turned into a normal five-year-old girl again. She ran to the wizard and apologised for being rude.

Danika Cosway-Richardson (9)
John Stocker Middle School, Devon

THE FOREST ON MISTY MOORS

Hi, my name is Becky and I live at home with my sisters, Jodie who is seven and Jessica who is eight. I'm ten. We live next door to our cousins, David and George, who are eight and nine. This year, we are all going on a holiday, camping on Dartmoor. Mum and Dad are busy packing things, so we have to stay out of their way. It's Saturday and we are on our way to Dartmoor. Jodie, Jess and I are playing I-spy to pass the time.

It's really nice as we approach the moor lands, the sun was drifting in and out of the heavy black clouds above. Mum and Dad started to put the tents up, so me, Jess, Jodie, David and George decided to have a look around. Not far from us, we spotted a large forest. It looked really interesting, but before we could get anywhere near the first trees, Mum told us that we shouldn't go in there. We set up a game of football instead, to try and resist the temptation to go in the forest. Unfortunately, the boys got a little carried away and kicked the ball right into the forest. David went to go and get it, but Jodie told him not to go. He didn't listen and walked straight past her. We couldn't leave him to go alone, so we hurried in after him.

The forest was dark and it had a funny smell around it. We all wondered what it was, but we couldn't place what it was. We all decided that it was a better idea just to get the ball and get out of there as fast as possible. None of us liked the forest and now that we were in it, it didn't seem all that interesting after all. Just really spooky. Suddenly, Jess gave a scream. We asked what was wrong and she said that she thought she saw a dark shape among the trees to our left. There was a large, old tree. At first, we couldn't see anything, but near the bottom of the tree, there was definitely something there. We tried to run, but as we turned, we noticed that the trees had either moved, or we'd gotten lost somehow. We couldn't find the way out! Then, all of a sudden, as we jumped through a large, ferny sort of plant, we found our ball lying on the forest floor. David ran to pick it up and as he did, he gave a shout. We'd found the edge of the forest.

Quickly, we ran back up the slope, back to our safe campsite. Back to Mum and Dad. Mum seemed really pleased to see us. She asked us where we had been. I said just in the field down there, playing football. I gave the others a look to make sure that they didn't say anything else.

The next day, we all got up early, the sense of adventure back, so we decided to go and have another look in the forest to see what it really was that had scared us out of our wits the day before. When we got there, we found a little hut that wasn't there before. We decided to have a little look. We were just looking in the window when a voice said, 'And what do you think you're doing?'
The voice made us all jump, but when we turned around, we saw a kind looking man. We told him we were on holiday and he said that he was on holiday too, although George didn't believe him. We stayed for a little while and then we said goodbye and went back to our tent. All of us had completely forgotten about the unusual figure in the woods, until we got back home. We thought that it would make quite a good story, so we decided to write it down. Here it is!

Rebecca Cohead (9)
John Stocker Middle School, Devon

A Bad Day For A Picnic

Once upon a time, seven little boys decided to go on a picnic in the forest. They all grouped up in pairs and went to have a play before lunch. When the oldest boy (who had set out the picnic) shouted out, 'Lunch is ready,' there was no reply.

The reason why there was no reply was because the first and second boys had climbed very tall trees and were too frightened to come down. The twins had gone rowing and the oars had dropped in the lake. They had to use their hands to paddle, which took a lot longer. The last two had gone for a paddle in a big pond. They found that it was a swamp and both got their legs totally stuck.

After ten minutes of waiting, the boy sighed and said, 'Oh well, more for me!' in a chuckling voice.

An hour later, they all came back, two by two. The twins were soaked, two were mucky and the other two were glad to have their feet on the ground. When they came to have a bite to eat, there wasn't a crumb left!

Jodie Brush (9)
John Stocker Middle School, Devon

GHOST WORLD

Once upon a time, a new world was discovered, towards the left of the universe. Nobody lived there. There were buildings and shops, but not a single soul in sight. When scientists went to discover this new world, the things in the buildings were moving and switching places.

Nothing was seen, but there was a sound. It sounded like a ghost. It sounded like it came from the floor underneath them. Then, not a single item moved, and not a single noise was heard, but there was definitely a noise before, so something definitely had been there. Some kind of creature had been in the buildings.

The scientists walked down to the doorway, as quiet as mice. There was a sign, it said, *Beware of Ghost!* The scientists ran as fast as they possibly could. They got into their rocket and headed for Earth at 459 miles per hour. They were there in no time at all.

When all the scientists came back from their experiment, they quickly rushed through the town to their lab. They explained all that had happened. Nobody denied the fact that they would never leave Earth again. They had never seen such a scary sight.

James Tylisczuk (9)
John Stocker Middle School, Devon

AMELIA'S WAR

Amelia cowered as the bombs whistled and fell. She could see the red glow over Exeter, where the Germans had dropped fire bombs. Another explosion made the house shake. Amelia dived under the grand piano and pulled the skirt across in front of her. She hoped to God that her mother was all right. Why had her mother chosen such a year of danger to stay with her sister in Exeter?

After hours of explosions, the bombs stopped. It was 2am. Amelia crawled out from under the piano and found that she was shaking with fear. She climbed into bed, but she couldn't get to sleep. Horrible visions danced through her head, all containing mangled corpses and ruined houses. She waited and waited, knowing that her mother was meant to be coming home that week. But her mother did not come. She tried not to give up hope, but it was virtually impossible.

Finally, after a week had passed, Amelia knew in her heart that her mother was dead. A huge hole opened up inside her, cutting her to pieces. She screamed the loudest scream she had ever screamed, tears streaming down her beautiful young face. She ripped the lace from her night-gown and set about destroying the house. Her mind had broken in her grief. And it had been one of the most intelligent minds in all of Devon. She ran from the house, wailing and shrieking like a hunted banshee.

Mrs Partridge, her next-door neighbour, looked out of her window to see what all the noise was. She didn't recognise Amelia, and raced to her cupboard. She drew out a blunderbuss. Shouting out, 'German scum! Take that!' she fired out of the window. She was rewarded by a shrill cry of pain. Satisfied, Mrs Partridge turned away from the window.

Behind the hill, Amelia crawled away, her leg bleeding freely. Visions danced across her dazed eyes. She didn't know where she was going, but something inside her told her just to lie down and fall into an eternal sleep. She fought against the urge for as long as she could, but in the end, she was too exhausted to fight anymore. She painfully crawled into a hollow and lay down. She piled leaves on top of her and took a last look around herself. For one fleeting moment, she thought she saw an angel, but then it was gone. Sighing a sigh as one who is sleeping peacefully after being tortured, she closed her eyes for what seemed like the final time.

Amelia's eyes fluttered open. She didn't know where she was. Four concerned faces, all sporting bristling moustaches, were looking at her. Then the angel appeared again. Seeing him closer, she saw that he was merely a handsome man, wearing a dark green uniform. A soldier. She glanced at her leg and saw that it was bound with a thick bandage. Exhausted, she fell back into sleep.

Amelia stayed in the sick bay of the army outpost for many weeks, growing more and more attached to the soldiers that were stationed there. They had been marching to their new base, when Peter, the angel-like soldier, had spotted her. They had carried her with them to their new base, where they had bound her. They grew so attached to her, it was decided that Amelia would stay with them for as long as she wished. Amelia, however, had more important things on her mind. Although she could not talk, she and Peter were in love. He had expressed his love for her five days after she came out of sick bay. She had not been able to return the feelings with words, but he understood.

Months passed and Amelia and Peter grew closer. Then the war reached them. The Germans had found the base, and had sent their bombers to destroy it. The soldiers escaped, bringing Amelia with them. It was only when they were outside that they realised that Peter was not with them. Amelia broke free of the soldiers' restraining hands and ran back into the base. She found Peter, trapped under a fallen beam. She tried to lift it, but it was too heavy. Amelia could hear the whistles of the new bombs as they fell. She had time to escape still, but instead, she simply laid her head on his crushed chest and waited. She heard the first bomb whistling even louder now that it was closer, and then it hit them.

Karen Elson (12)
John Stocker Middle School, Devon

Lucy's Surprise

A girl called Lucy lived with her auntie as her mum and dad had died. Lucy hated her auntie as she was horrible to her. Her only friends were a cuddly cat and a doll that her mum and dad had given her.

Lucy was about to go to sleep. She talked to the cat like she always did, but that night the cat came to life. The cat said, 'Hello Lucy, would you like to go on adventure?'
'Where to?' said Lucy.
'Wherever you want to go,' answered the cat.
'That's easy,' said Lucy, 'to Chocolate Land.'
'Climb on my back and I will take you to Chocolate Land, said the cat.

People ate chocolate while they were walking around. The buildings were made of chocolate, the river was made of chocolate. The lamps were made of candyfloss. Doors and windows were made of candy. Lucy put some chocolate in her dressing gown pocket for later.

Next morning, Lucy put on her dressing gown and went downstairs and thought about the wonderful dream she had. She took her tissue out of her pocket, but found a chocolate bar. She ran back to her room and the cat winked at her.

Lucy Roke (9)
John Stocker Middle School, Devon

FRIENDS FOREVER

Sarah woke up, it was the holidays. She felt so happy, she went downstairs at 6:30 in the morning! But then the smile on her face was wiped away. She wanted Hollie, just Hollie. They had fallen out on the last day of school. She ran out of the front door, still in her pyjamas 'Hollie!'

Hollie looked out of her window. She thought, no, yes. It was Sarah. She ran all the way downstairs and out of the door in a second. She shouted, 'Sarah!'
Sarah shouted back, 'Hollie!'
Then they ran to each other. Sarah said, 'Sorry, sorry, sorry.'
Hollie replied, 'Sorry, sorry too.'
Then both said, 'We shall be friends forever.'

Sarah Chakmakchi (9)
John Stocker Middle School, Devon

Spunky And The Magic Tree

Once there lived two dogs called Spunky and Sarge, they loved to play with each other. One day, Sarge said, 'Let's go to the woods.' Spunky said that he was too scared to go. 'There's nothing to be scared of,' said Sarge.'
'B-B-But there's Hufferlumps and Woozles,' said Spunky.
Sarge said, 'Come on, stay close to me.' But as usual, Spunky didn't for long, he got scared and ran off.

Spunky stopped running because he was tired. He sat down to rest by a tree. Suddenly, strange sparkles came from a hole in the tree. Spunky climbed into the hole. He slid down and down and landed on a soft piece of grass. There was a dog named Dog Dickens. Dog Dickens said, 'Who are you?'
'My name is Spunky.'

Dog Dickens showed Spunky around his land. It was a lovely sunny day, so they had a picnic. When Spunky was about to eat a sandwich, he shot into the air, going higher and higher, spinning as he went. All he could hear was his name, 'Spunky! Spunky!' Spunky looked up and saw Sarge looking at him. 'Wake up, you've been dreaming,' said Sarge.
'Just get me out of here,' said Spunky, and off they ran.

Rebecca Webb (9)
John Stocker Middle School, Devon

The Nightmares

One day I was in a van to pick up some wood for Dad and we went to a wood shop near Exmouth. Once we got there, we got out of the van and went in the shop. There was this long queue, nearly going outside the shop.

I was nearly at the counter, but this man had a long list of things he wanted. He took ten minutes. When it was our turn, we ordered some cherry wood and some paint, because it was on special offer and he was running out of it. The man said, 'We haven't got any wood or paint,' and ran after us.

'Aaaaah! Good, it's a dream.' It was 7 o'clock, time to get up. I went downstairs and looked out of the window. I knew it was June, so I expected a sunny day, but it was snowing and my brother came in and said, 'Robert!' And then I woke up.

Robert Browning (9)
John Stocker Middle School, Devon

THE MIRROR PUDDLE

Carrie was walking home down the muddy lane, as the rain soaked through her jumper. Suddenly, she tripped on a small twig and before realising it, had fallen in a deep puddle. She looked up. To see her reflection was horrible! She was covered head to toe in mud. Because she was a princess this didn't look good!

Then, the puddle changed - it was no longer a murky grey, but a clear picture lay there! Carrie's parents sat on high seats, watching her. She was dancing! She was dancing with a young, wealthy man about her age. Suddenly, a huge grey monster towered over him, and with huge teeth - bit off his head!

Scared to death, Carrie ran home.

The next day, her mother announced, 'There is to be a young prince coming to the palace.' Carrie jumped for joy, then remembered the puddle - *Was it warning her?*

Later that day he arrived. He was tall and proud, yet polite and friendly. They danced. Then, Carrie saw it.
Huge and scaly with four long legs. Carrie tried to scream, but nothing came out. This had to happen. It was *meant* to happen.

She woke up with tears in her eyes.

Eleanor Spencer (9)
John Stocker Middle School, Devon

THE LITTLE FISH

Hi, I'm Fin. Welcome to my home, Goldfish Road, which I love. I don't like school because there are five bullies called Rainbow, Gil, Texas, James and Rex. At break time, they bullied the little fish like me. If anyone stands up to them, they will beat them up.

One day, the bullies were in a mean mood. Lucy, my friend, was playing with the other girls. She bumped into the bullies who were talking close to the girls. They attacked Lucy, who tried to fight back, but couldn't. I tried to comfort her, she was shaking like a jellyfish. No one seemed to be able to help.

We decided to get our own back. Our plan was simple, we decided to throw vegetables at them. We hid and waited for them. When we caught sight of them, I shouted, 'Ready, aim, *fire!*'

It worked. They are no longer bullies. We all became friends and lived happily ever after.

Bethany Connett (9)
John Stocker Middle School, Devon

JASMINE'S ADVENTURE

It was the beginning of the summer holidays. Jasmine was excited as the family were getting a car, at last!

In the car, Jasmine fell asleep. Her parents left her in the car. When she woke up, she was in a strange land. Roman soldiers marched, shouting, 'Sin dex! Sin dex!' Their clanking metal discs and stamping feet in studded sandals made such a racket!

Feeling confused, Jasmine wandered into a hut where she was offered stuffed dormouse. Whilst she tried to get out, a Roman centurion blocked her way, bellowing, 'Money, Jasius!' Frightened, Jasmine ran like the wind back to the car. When she noticed Roman soldiers stampeding towards her, her eyes popped out of her head. What was happening?

Jasmine threw herself into the driving seat and turned the ignition key. Nothing happened. The soldiers were close. Her heart pounded in her throat. Sweaty palms meant the keys slipped, but Jasmine managed to turn the key. The engine roared! Green mist surrounded her. When it cleared, Jasmine was back outside her home. Her parents got into the car. 'Hi, Darling! Had a nice kip?' asked Mum. Dad started to turn the ignition key.

'No!' cried Jasmine.

Jasmine Davey (9)
John Stocker Middle School, Devon

THE SCARY STORY

Chapter 1 The Fete.

Once upon a time there was a ghost called Will and he had two very good friends called Jack and Hannah. They all lived in a house on the edge of a village called Ide.

One fine summer's day, Will woke up and went to the village fete with Hannah and Jack. When they got there, Jack looked round and saw a weird, mysterious woman. She was dressed all in purple with a large, pointy hat and flying around the hat were coloured stars and red and blue bats.

Hannah and Jack wanted to go and talk to the woman, but Will told them that they had to find out her name first. 'How are we going to do that if we do not ask her?' said Jack.
'Well,' said Will, 'we have to catch a bat.'
'How?' said Hannah, looking into the woman's dark, scary, red eyes.
'Don't worry, as a ghost I can change into a bat and bring one back in my bat pack, but we have to get the right one. If we don't, then the woman will turn all the villagers into stone.'

So off he went in a puff of dust. Jack and Hannah were playing on the bouncy castle and there was a big *flash, bang* and everyone was like a statue, apart from Jack and Hannah.

To be continued . . .

Mark Foster (9)
John Stocker Middle School, Devon

Jessica's Curiosity

Once upon a time, there was a girl called Jessica and she went to a school called Lucky Junior High. One day, she was walking home from school and saw something curling its finger, telling her to come over to a spooky old house. Jessica walked to the house. Whilst she was standing by the house, Jessica thought she may as well go in.

Jessica went into the house and saw some stairs. She took one step, making a loud noise, so all the rats that had infested the house squealed and ran around. Jessica continued up the stairs, frightened, and came to a door. There she discovered a playroom and a beautiful china doll. She picked it up and closely inspected it.

Suddenly, a grotesque spider crawled from behind the doll and scared her. Rats downstairs and spiders upstairs scared Jessica so much that she thought the best thing to do was leave as soon as possible. She ran, with the doll in her hands, and escaped through a fire exit. She was very lucky, because the building was a deserted orphanage.

Jessica ran home as fast as she could and thought to herself, I'm never going there again.

Emily Shields (10)
Manor House School, Devon

HAUNTED HOUSE

It was our first day at our new house. I had been unpacking all day, so I was practically dead. I went to bed and I was just falling asleep, when I heard a weird sound. It was like a moaning noise and it seemed like it was in the room next door to me, but that would be impossible because there is no room next to me.

I got out of bed and went to see what it was. I couldn't see anything, so I turned around and went back. I opened the door and the hair on my neck stood up. There was a white figure standing right in front of me. I was frozen with fear, so I slowly stepped back and then I ran as fast as I could to the sitting room, where Mum and Dad were still unpacking boxes. I ran to them and told them what had happened. I don't' think they believed me, but they came up with me anyway.

In the morning when we were having breakfast, I heard my mum say, 'I'm sure I put the fruit bowl over there yesterday.' I smiled and carried on eating my breakfast.

Georgina Hunt (9)
Manor House School, Devon

NOT QUITE WHAT YOU REMEMBER

I was happy, I was back at home where I belonged. The big old house with its once beautiful gardens and orchard, its vast acres of land, where ponies once stood, placed in the middle of nowhere. As I walked in the shadow of the big old house, I listened to the songs of the birds high in the trees.

I walked up round the edge of my favourite field, the one with the old stables and the old Roman road. I felt happier than I had in days, knowing I was back where I belonged, walking on the firm ground that my ancestors had left me.

I soon reached the old Roman road, but I stopped dead. (I had heard the stories, but I never dreamt they were true.) I could see people, pure white people, white as snow, walking and talking in a far-off voice I could not make out.

That night while in bed, I thought, did I really see what I think I saw? I had been up there hundreds of times before, but I had never seen anything like that before. Were the ancestors' stories really true, and were the ghosts of horses up in the old stables that had not been used for centuries? Then I fell asleep, puzzling over everything I had seen that day.

Harriet Carr (11)
Manor House School, Devon

A Midnight Stroll

A black cat entered the garden, no one knew he was there. He crept through the dewy grass that came up to his knees. With an enormous leap, he scrambled up the trunk of a tree and along a thin branch. He sat there contemplating what to do next, as he watched the rest of the garden. With no warning, he jumped down from the tree and crossed the garden and slunk up the path with his tail in the air. He leapt over the low garden wall and disappeared into the night. The only sign of the cat was the footprints, delicately stamped into the grass.

Katya Moore (11)
Manor House School, Devon

THE HAUNTED HOUSE

On one stormy night, two children looked out of their window and saw a gloomy well out in the garden. One of the children, who was called David, said, 'Shall we go down the well?'
'Yes,' said Luke.
'Let's go!' said David.

The two boys climbed carefully down the steps into the well. At the bottom of the steps, David saw a group of bats flying towards them. David said, 'Run!' David and Luke headed along the passageway until they reached some more steps.
'The only way is up,' said Luke, pointing to the steps.
As they climbed the steps, David said, 'Look, it's a house. Let's look around.'

Luke was scared, but David said, 'Come on, don't be a chicken!' David opened a trapdoor into the dining room.
Luke said, 'Look, there's slime hanging from the ceiling!'
And then David said, 'Look, are those zombies and vampires coming towards us?'
'Yes,' said Luke, trembling . . .

Sam Kallaway (9)
Manor House School, Devon

THE LONELY GHOST

It was raining and I was bored, so I decided to explore the cellar. It was cold and dark so I switched on the light. In the middle of the floor stood a ghost!

'Aarghhh!' I yelled.
'Aarghhh!' yelled the ghost and disappeared.
'Sorry I frightened you,' I called into the empty room, 'but I didn't expect a ghost in the cellar. Please come back. What's your name?'
'Thomas,' said the ghost reappearing, 'and I'm lonely, I need to find a haunted house. I'm too young to haunt alone.'
'You're in luck,' I said. 'There's an empty haunted house at the end of the village. I'll take you there.'

As we walked through the village, Thomas floated through parked cars and lamp posts. When we arrived at the gloomy old house, he asked me to go inside. It didn't look very inviting, but I followed him through a broken window.

Inside, there were other ghosts and they were having a party and Thomas looked so happy, I slipped away before they noticed me. Climbing through the window, I looked back and smiled at Thomas, who waved before going off to play hide-and-seek with his new friends.

Harry Edmanson (11)
Manor House School, Devon

BEACH ADVENTURE

One day, two boys called James and Tom were walking along a beach. When they were walking, Tom spotted a cave with diamonds around the sides. They decided to go in.

The boys eventually came to a dead end and lying there was a big, huge troll. The troll lay there asleep. He was snoring as loud as my dad!

They chose to go back, but the only way back was blocked by a wall, so they couldn't get out. To open the door, the only way out was to pull a lever behind the troll. They pulled the lever, then ran through the door.

The lever had also opened a treasure box that they took home. Inside, they found a life supply of sweets!

Christopher Pomeroy (10)
Manor House School, Devon

GREAT AUNT MAGGIE'S GHOST

The first night I stayed with Great Aunt Maggie in her tumble-down Victorian mansion, things began to go wrong. My Game Boy went missing.

I was sleeping at the top of the house in a little wood-panelled room. It was so far up, that my Great Aunt couldn't even climb the stairs, so she couldn't have taken it.

The next night my watch vanished and I could hear creaking floorboards and faint footsteps creeping around the room. By the time I'd been there a week, I was so terrified I asked my great aunt if I could change bedrooms, and so I moved into the room next to hers. Everything seemed quite normal, but I still hadn't found my things.

Two weeks after I got home, Great Aunt Maggie wrote, saying she had just had a terrible shock. When she was getting a bottle of wine from the cellar, she had seen a strange man, wearing a top hat, a long jacket and my watch. He was staring at a weird purple gadget which had a small screen and grey buttons on the front. And then he had just vanished through the wall.

Alex Macadam (10)
Manor House School, Devon

WHAT A SHOT

One day, a boy called James was watching his favourite football team (Newcastle) play Man U. At half-time, an advert said that one lucky ten-year-old would be able to meet and play with the Newcastle squad on the 15th April against Liverpool. When James heard that, he instantly answered the question and phoned the number on the screen.

A week later, James received a letter saying that he would play with Newcastle on Saturday, the 15th April against Liverpool. The next day, James and his family travelled to Newcastle to get ready for the match.

The day came and James was going to be the second striker. When James found out that there were 60,000 supporters, he almost fainted! The game started and the crowd cheered. It sounded like a rodeo, but the cheering was much louder! At half-time, the score was 0-0 and Michael Owen had been sent off.

The second half started and Newcastle got off to a great start. After 85 minutes of the game, Newcastle made a substitution and Kieron Dyer came off to be replaced by Lua Lua. There were two minutes left and James had the ball. He dribbled it to the halfway line and took a shot. The ball shot into the air and flew past the goalkeeper. The score was 1-0 to Newcastle and they had won!

James Welch-Thornton (10)
Manor House School, Devon

OCTOBER 31ST

Once there were two children called Emily and Holly. They were both ten and very nosy. They had always been curious about a house at the end of their road. One stormy afternoon, they decided to look inside the creepy house.

They opened the door, it squeaked like a mouse when you had just stepped on his tail, they went upstairs and looked in the bedrooms. There was nothing there. 'Disappointing really,' said Emily.

They looked downstairs and saw the biggest saucepan they had ever seen in the kitchen. They heard a scratching behind a cupboard door. They opened it and screamed as a big black cat lurched out at them.

As they picked themselves up from the floor, they discovered whoever lived there wasn't very house proud. There were cobwebs everywhere! They were covered in dust! All of a sudden, Emily said, 'Can you hear that? Listen.'
'Hubble bubble, toil and trouble, I know two girls who are in big trouble.'
They looked at each other and ran from the house. 'I'm never going there again,' said Emily.
'Neither am I,' said Holly.

The lonely old woman watched them running away, laughing to herself. Every year they come looking and end up running away. Chickens!

Holly Ford (10)
Manor House School, Devon

THE MUMMY

One day in Egypt, there were two people called Jane and Chris. They arrived in a plane. First, they got their equipment out, then they got into the Land Rover. They made their way to the pyramids and after a while, their Land Rover broke down.

Jane was walking around when suddenly, she got sucked underground. Then Chris was sucked down with her. They had discovered an underground room. Jane saw a passage going down. They both started to walk down the passage and then suddenly, they saw a mummy. It saw them and it started to walk closer and closer.

The mummy's body had all rotted away. Chris got his pistol out and started to fire. Bits of flesh spurted out as Chris was firing the pistol, then it hit Jane against the wall. The mummy started to retreat. Chris went to see if Jane was all right. She was dead.

Chris started to walk through the passage. Suddenly flying arrows came and he quickly ducked and carried on. Then the mummy came again and whacked him against the wall and made a hole in the wall. It started to retreat.

The army had come because Chris had called them on his phone, and Chris survived.

Harry Lawrence (10)
Manor House School, Devon

THE JUNGLE LAW

In the jungle, two animals stood talking about Sinders. Sinders was a snake, a foul, cold, evil and cruel snake that was hated by all the animals who lived in the jungle, but he was hated most by Leo the lion and Mickey, the monkey. Their hatred for him was matched by loathing for them and every other animal in the jungle.

In the end, Leo and the other animals got together to form a law that, if you break it, a spell gets put on you so that you get turned into apple pie. So they sent pieces of parchment to everybody in the jungle, including Sinders. Sinders ignored it and threw it into the fire.

The next day, Sinders went into the jungle and broke the law by nicking Leo's toy. A fairy was summoned at once and Sinders became an apple pie, and to this day, the jungle law still remains a big scare to all the people in the jungle. That is if you have not been turned into a pie.

Oliver Persey (10)
Manor House School, Devon

THE TIME MACHINE

Roar! The beast trudged away over the moor. Mark was watching television. Mark like everything about beasts.

That night, Mark went out with his dad. He looked up at the sky. Suddenly, something shot across the sky and disappeared. 'Hey! What was that?' he cried.
'You must have seen a shooting star,' said his dad. 'Quick, make a wish!'
Mark wished he could see what it was like to be standing in the world of beasts.

Soon it was time to go to bed. Mark fell asleep quite quickly after his long star-watch. Suddenly, Mark heard a strange whirring sound outside. He went to the window and saw something looking like a grandfather clock standing outside. He went out into the garden and opened it. It was huge inside! Then, the clock started whirring again.

When the whirring stopped, Mark opened the door. He was amazed that he was standing in moor land. Suddenly, he heard a roar. He turned around and saw a huge beast walking towards him. Then, he noticed there were lots of other beasts around. He jumped back into the time-machine and went home.

He woke up in bed and wondered if it was a dream. But his wish had come true.

Isobel Caton Harrison (9)
Manor House School, Devon

ALEX AND THE FOX

Once there lived a boy called Alex. One day, he went for a walk in the woods. Suddenly, he noticed a small fox sitting on a rock. If an animal could cry, he would have sworn it was crying. Very slowly, he moved towards it, tiptoe by tiptoe. He stretched out to stroke it and the fox didn't mind.

Alex was about to walk away when the fox spoke. 'Don't go.'
At first, Alex thought he was dreaming. 'Was that you?' he whispered.
He was sure it wouldn't' answer, but then a voice said, 'Please don't leave me.'
'What's wrong?'
So the fox told him how his mother had been shot and there was no one to look after him. Presently, Alex said, 'Would you like to come home with me? I'll look after you.'
'Oh yes!' said the fox.
'Only you must promise never to eat my mum's chickens or talk in front of other humans. If you do, they will take you away and put you in the circus.'
'I promise,' said the fox.
And so the fox went home with Alex and from that day, they were never apart.

'You'd think they could talk to each other,' giggled Alex's mum. Little did she know!

Thomas Auckland (11)
Manor House School, Devon

MY BEST DAY OUT

I had just woken up and remembered that I was going to Woodlands. I had been there before and never wanted to leave. So I got out of bed, got dressed and ran downstairs to have breakfast, eating as much as I could because I knew I was going to be busy doing lots of things!

I got into Dad's new car and drove off to Woodlands. It takes one and a half hours, so I took my Game Boy and played Space Invaders. At last we had arrived, I couldn't wait to go on my favourite ride, The Toboggan. I raced off to join the queue, but to my amazement, there were hardly any people in the queue. I waited in the queue with about ten people. Then I felt someone tap me on the shoulder. It was my friend Josh. I asked him if he wanted to go on with me and he said yes. We waited for two minutes, then it was our turn. The chain pulled us slowly up to the slope. At the top, we let go of the brake and went zooming down!

It as even better than I remembered!

Tom Vanstone (11)
Manor House School, Devon

UPSTAIRS

Any minute now, the dreaded words would come . . .
'Time for bed,' said Mum.
And however much she dragged her feet, however long it took to fill her water glass, however many times she pretended she had lost her pyjamas, however slowly she said goodnight, sooner or later she would have to go up those stairs. 'Can't I have just five more minutes?' Laura said desperately.
'No, I want to watch my TV programme, so hurry up.'

Laura looked gloomily up the stairs. She shuffled towards them as slowly as she could. She knew what was waiting at the top. Eyes staring at her from all sides, invisible ghosts talking to her in strange, bitter voices, faces laughing and smirking at her, the curtains twitching and who knows what behind them.

Laura took a deep breath and walked up the stairs. When she reached the top, Laura sat down hoping her mum would call her down again, but she heard nothing. Eventually, she stood up and clasped the door handle. Slowly, the knob turned until the door creaked open. Her heart thumping, Laura reached for the light switch. She forced her eyes open and saw . . . absolutely nothing!

Cressida Auckland (9)
Manor House School, Devon

FANTASTIC FOOTBALLER

Fantastic Footballer was off to watch his reserve team play. 'I wonder if they're getting better?' he said to himself. But when he got there, he took one glance and said, 'Er, probably not.' They were about the same size as baby elephants.

So, the match started and to tell you the truth, they couldn't tackle fish and chips. With it being 21-2 at half-time, there was no chance of winning. At one point, the ball got stuck under Smudger's (the winger) shirt. At the end of the game, it was 42-4.

Fantastic Footballer went to Burgers 'R' Us, but when he sat down, the waitress came over to him and said, 'I'm sorry, you can't sit there. It's reserved.'
'Who for?' FF replied.
'Your reserves,' the waitress explained.
'What!' FF shouted. So he went out in a strop.

Matthew Hutchings (10)
Manor House School, Devon

CATCH THE THIEF

Liz's new jumper had been stolen and so had a number of other items around the small town.

Liz had just come home from school and was sitting in the park with her best friend, Jamie. Liz stood up saying, 'I'm off to find this clever thief. Come on Jamie.' They set of to Mr Ben's old, dusty tool shop. He was their prime suspect, who always looked rather suspicious around the town.

Near the old shop, Jamie drew a sharp breath and stumbled over an uneven drain. 'That never used to be there,' said Jamie crossly as he picked himself up.

Unfortunately, the tool shop was shut. As they returned and stepped over the drain, they noticed it had twisted round, so both children were puzzled. They walked on and luckily met Mr Ben, but to their disappointment, he said that he had no connection with the criminal. So the children came to a conclusion.

They hid behind a dense bush and watched Mr Ben's shop, but to their astonishment, a young man dressed in black hurried down the drain with some stolen goods. The excited children ran and shut the drain, trapping the thief. Then they ran to tell the police, relieved that Mr Ben was innocent.

Jocelyn Trayler-Clarke (11)
Manor House School, Devon

A Day In The Life Of A Mountain Guide

I wake up and the icy wind whistles through my tent. Day has just broken over the Austrian Alps. I get out of my sleeping bag and get into my mountaineering clothes. I get out of my tent to wake my party of nine up to have breakfast and get to the next waypoint. Everyone eats and then we all have to pack up our tents (which I can tell you is quite tough), put all our gear into our rucksacks and link up a rope between us, so we don't lose anyone, and go.

After about an hour and a half, as I'm walking along poking my ice axe in front of me, with no warning, my ice axe finds a depression and the ice and snow in front of me falls 100 feet down a crevasse. I tell everyone to get out a tent and cook a snack while I get across it. So I abseil down one side and climb up the other.

At the top, I set up a zip wire. When everyone is over, we set off again until lunch. After three hours, we stop and have lunch. One of the older people was fatigued, so we stop for the night. Everyone gets out their tents. After seven hours of eating and talking, we all go to sleep.

Ben Matthews (11)
Manor House School, Devon

THE NETBALL MATCH

I'd just moved house in a friendly little village, when something really odd happened to me.

The third day that I'd been living in my new house, I went off to explore and make some friends around our village. It was a warm summer's day and there were lots of flowers out. I could hear some birds singing softly.

I looked round a very big, old building which had lots of windows. I heard lots of laughter echoing round its big walls and whoever it was, they seemed to be having a lot of fun! There in front of me were about twenty odd-looking girls, all playing together, who all looked like sisters to me. They walked up to me and started checking out my clothes. They were wearing unusual uniforms for some unknown reason and some really weird shoes.

After introducing myself, we went to an old netball court and started to play netball with a battered ball. I had a great time and they said I was really good.

About a week later, we went to visit our next-door neighbour, Margaret, and I told her all about the group of girls. She gave me a strange look and told me that a girls' school used to stand there, but it was bombed in the war and twenty girls were killed . . .

Kate Edwards (11)
Manor House School, Devon

A Day In The Life Of The Queen

Hello, I am Elizabeth II. Many of you know me as the Queen of the United Kingdom. I am sitting on my throne and I am about to tell you about an average day in the life of . . . yes, you've guessed it. Me!

It is Friday, the 16th of August. After a long, tiring night, I woke up and this is where the story starts! I woke up and there in front of me was breakfast in bed, brought up by one of the maids.

This morning, I am going to have a meeting with President Bush to discuss what's going to happen in Afghanistan. A few hours later, we leave the meeting and I go back to my palace. It is lunchtime and Prince Charles and I have a nice prawn curry.

After lunch, I take my corgis for a walk, then I go back to the palace and have dinner. I watch EastEnders, then I go to bed.

Camilla Fisher Crouch (9)
Manor House School, Devon

THE UNDERGROUND TUNNEL

Once there was a boy named Tom. He had brown hair, blue eyes and he was eight years old. One day, he went walking in the forest nearby. While he was walking along, Tom tripped up on a tree root. When he woke up, he found himself in a pit. He stood up and tried to climb up the wall, but it was no use.

Then he looked around and saw a door. He walked up to the door and opened it. When he got in, he heard a loud slam! The door had shut behind him. Then he turned around and tried to open the door, but it was too hard, so he had to go through the tunnel.

Tom did not want to go into the dark, dim tunnel. He entered slowly, he was shaking, when suddenly a gargoyle jumped up behind him. He picked up a stick and whacked the gargoyle to the floor. Tom walked on and saw a pile of old things. In the pile, there was a glow of gold. He went over and picked up the handle and found out it was a sword. It was a big, long golden sword, made out of pure gold.

As Tom looked at the sword, he felt something around his legs and looked down. It was a giant snake with bright red skin. With one slash of the sword, Tom chopped the snake's head off. He was free! He ran, he met zombies and skeletons, he was petrified. He ran until he saw light and a long ladder. He scrambled up it. He was free at last and the sword was his trophy.

Freddie Galley (8)
Manor House School, Devon

THE MUSEUM

One day, a boy called Jake was really excited because he was going to the museum near his home in Colyford. So off they went in the car to the museum. When they arrived, Jake jumped out of the car and ran to the pillars. While his mum was paying, Jake wandered off to have a look around.

He saw a castle that wasn't there the last time he went, so Jake walked closer. His heart suddenly started beating faster and faster. As he got closer, he saw a trapdoor. He heard a noise and stood there like a statue. A mummy in a glass case had winked at him. Jake's heart stopped beating for a moment, he thought he could not move. He was so shocked! He knew what he had seen, but who would believe him? There was nobody in the room. Jake was scared. Then he heard his mum's voice, 'Why are you in the theatre?' Jake looked around and realised that by accident, he had walked into the theatre next door to the museum. The mummy that winked at Jake was an actor and the castle was a prop so he ran out of the room, very embarrassed.

Kit Kelsey (9)
Manor House School, Devon

GHOST STORY

One morning, there was a girl named Jessica who had a dog called Zip Zap. Jessica went into the woods and it was spooky. Jessica heard footsteps behind her; she turned around and nothing was there. She carried on walking. She turned again and she saw a man with goggly eyes. The man said, 'Who are you?'
'I'm . . . I'm . . . called J-J-Jessica. Who are you?'
'I'm an alien, come down from space.'

Jessica turned around and carried on walking. She suddenly stopped, something was wrong. She felt something crawling up her back, it was a spider.

She went on and heard people. There was a house. Not just a real house, a haunted house with damaged windows, cobwebs, creepy-crawlies, all sorts of disgusting things.

Jessica crept forward, she saw something black. It was a black cat! She moved forward again and again, until she finally discovered a man. She opened the door and there was spooky stuff everywhere. Jessica thought to herself and said, 'Don't be scared.' She walked on through the house. She reached the top and saw loads more people. She saw about twenty more people! She went downstairs again and she went outside and carried on walking, until she came to a dead end, where she saw a row of demons. They were guarding something, thought Jessica.

She tried to barge through them but she couldn't, she wasn't strong enough to see what they were guarding. She tried and tried, but she couldn't do it. She got out of the dead end and went back to the haunted house. She went back up to the room with the people in and spoke to them. They said nothing. She realised that they were vampires! She quickly ran out of the room with the vampires chasing her!

Gaby Fielding (9)
Manor House School, Devon

DOGGIE ADVENTURE

When I woke, I felt a tingling in my paws and I knew I would have an adventure.

After breakfast, I jumped over the wall at the bottom of our garden and into the fields. It felt lovely running in the long, wet grass. Suddenly I saw something moving very quickly, it was a rabbit. Time for a game of chase. I ran and ran after the rabbit into a wood. Under the trees it was darker and the rabbit disappeared into a carpet of bluebells. Still looking for the rabbit, I found myself falling into a deep, dark hole.

I soon realised that I wasn't hurt, but how was I going to get out? I felt scared, but what was that over there? It was a tunnel. I went down the tunnel, sniffing as I went. Something smelt tasty. I came to a cave, full of - yes, it was full - of bones! What's that? A big, fat ginger cat. I tried to take a bone, but the cat hissed and tried to scratch me. What could I do?

I heard a sound, it was the fridge opening. Oh phew! I'm in my basket. It was all a dream.

Kirstin Maclean (8)
Manor House School, Devon

JOURNEY TO A NEW LAND

Michael lived in the land of Driodor. His mother had asked him to get a loaf of bread. On his way to buy the bread, he passed a newspaper stall. One of the newspapers contained the headline, 'This world we live on is about to be destroyed by a volcano in a month's time.' He stared, wide-eyed at the newspaper and read on. 'A ship called Grand Tiger is taking settlers and warriors to a new planet.'

Michael decided to join the warriors. He was chosen to fight in a sword fighting competition. He was fighting against the best boy in the group. Michael nearly gave the other boy a blow on the chest. Then the other boy narrowly missed Michael. The boy kept holding his sword up in the air, so Michael struck him on the leg. As both boys wore protective clothing, no harm was done. The teacher congratulated Michael on winning and said he could be a warrior on the new planet.

The next day, Michael set off for the new planet. Grand Tiger arrived in about two hours. They thought the planet was habitable and sent Grand Tiger back, so they could take all the other Earth-people to this new world. Michael woke early so he could guard the new planet. Then suddenly, he looked all around and saw aliens coming towards him. He drew his sword when the alien king was in front of him. The alien king said, 'We do not want battle, we want to live in your houses because ours have diseases and stale food.'

So Michael told all the people and discussed matters. The people said, 'Fine with us.'

The alien king lived in Michael's house and the humans lived in harmony with the aliens. Earth was destroyed by the volcano, but the Earth-people of Driodor lived on.

Demelza Trezise (8)
Manor House School, Devon

Moving House

In a dark hole in a tree, lived a bird who suddenly woke up. He got up and shook his black, silky feathers. He looked up at his old oak tree and thought to himself, time to find a new home and perhaps some new friends. He said goodbye to his old tree and set off on his journey.

He flew over miles and miles of countryside. As he did, he saw cows and sheep grazing. There were also rabbits happily hopping and jumping into their holes. He saw trains whizzing at high speeds below. Then he saw a big city with tall skyscrapers and huge town houses. He thought to himself, I don't think I can make a home here, so he flew on.

He flew on and found himself at the seaside. There were huge waves and the sea was very rough. He saw people building sandcastles and people screaming. He decided it wasn't the right place.

He saw the River Exe and beside it was a lovely wood. He decided to go down and have a closer look. There he found a large ash tree and thought that he could make a home there. After a few days, he had made some new friends to play with up in the sky.

Beth Luxton (8)
Manor House School, Devon

THE TALE OF KIT KITTEN

One day, Kit Kitten was walking along the road, when out popped Mr Badger from his hole and said, 'There's a flood ahead.'
Kit replied, 'Then how am I supposed to get home?'
Badger replied, 'Over the bridge, that's the way you should go home.'

On Kit went. He was walking through the long grass when suddenly, Mr Fox jumped out at him and chased him to the wooden bridge. Kit got his foot stuck in the rotten wood.
Mr Fox said, 'I'm going to eat you.'
Kit replied, 'Please don't eat me!'

Mr Fox could hear Kit's heart pounding like a big, bass drum. Kit really thought Mr Fox was going to eat him. As if by magic, he heard a rustle in the rushes down below the bridge and he saw two long brown ears appearing. He recognised that the ears belonged to his friend, Mr Tom Rabbit . . .

Eddie Morrison (9)
Manor House School, Devon

GHOST STORY

Once upon a time, there was a young boy called Tom. It was a fine evening and Tom decided to go for a walk in the woods. When he got to the dark woods, it was very quiet, then an owl flew over his head. Tom gave out a shriek and ran and ran, until he stopped and ended up next to a castle.

When he saw the castle, he said to himself, 'I think I should go and explore it.' So he did. Tom walked up to the huge gates. He walked in and stepped onto a creaky floorboard, which made a group of bats flutter around. Tom was very scared now. He knew he had to get out of there, but how?

William Mostyn (9)
Manor House School, Devon

AN ADVENTURE ON THE BEACH

It was a bright, sunny, summer's day and I was walking along the beach with my friend, Mark, when we came to a dark, mysterious looking cave. We went inside the cave. It was dark and spooky. There were spiders' webs with flies caught in them, wriggling around trying to escape.

The cave felt damp, scary and cold. There was a strong, funny-looking rock with fungus growing around it. Suddenly, we heard a loud and unhappy groaning sound coming from behind the rock. 'What on earth was that?' cried Mark.
'Shh. I don't know. What was that?'
We both crept quietly towards the rock. We peeped over the top and saw a gigantic red dragon, he was crying in pain. 'What is the matter?' I asked.
'It is my foot, there I something stuck in it. Please help!'
'Do you promise not to hurt us?'
'I promise I won't hurt you, and if you help me, I will take you on a magical ride.'
'Well, of course we will help you.'

We carefully stepped forward and looked at his foot. There was a sharp, jagged piece of glass caught in-between two toes.
'Take a deep breath.' We pulled hard and the glass came out.
'Ahhh!' cried the dragon. 'That feels much better. Hop onto my back.'

The next moment we were flying higher and higher over the sandy beach and right over the sea. He took us to the dragon land. All the dragons there were different colours. They were all very friendly to us and made us a wonderful feast. We had dancing and games and lots of fun.

Just before dark, the dragon flew us back to the beach. We ran all the way home and told our mums that we had had the best adventure in the world!

Charlie Pepworth (8)
Manor House School, Devon

THE TWO SPOTTED LADYBIRDS

Once upon a time there were two spotted ladybirds. Their names were Spot and Ready. Ready was a big ladybird and Spot was a tiny ladybird.

On the 23rd March it was competition day, when the two ladybirds race each other to see who can catch the most aphids. They can catch big ones, small ones and coloured ones.

Weeks and weeks went by until the day of the competition. The two ladybirds got up early to start the race. They went into the garden together, ready to start. Spot said, 'On your marks, get set, *go!*' By half-time, the two ladybirds had found two aphids each. Spot had two big aphids and Ready had found two small aphids . . .

Emma Hurford (9)
Manor House School, Devon

THE MYSTERY OF SCARY HILL

One morning I got up, it was a bank holiday. I woke my brother and we went downstairs. Suddenly, we heard a *bang!* We ran outside with our brand new slippers on, we knew Mum would go mad.

We went to the field. My brother jumped suddenly. For a few seconds, it was a complete blur. He was about to crash. I grabbed onto his leg. The horse kicked him into the muck heap just as Mummy came round.

My brother had to have a bath and you don't want to know what the water looked like. The pony was caught in the end.

After my brother had gotten out of the bath, we went down to the woods of Scary Hill. My grandma used to live there, but now she was dead. Back at home, Mummy was washing our slippers. We walked along the path to Grandma's house. We were just about to reach the house, when suddenly it disappeared and in its place, was our grandma! We were delighted. She showed us some of the wood. Suddenly, we fell onto our house and we all lived happily ever after.

Calista Trayler-Clarke (7)
Manor House School, Devon

MISTER DOG

I hate this, I really do. That stupid girl Pansy is plaiting my hair like a doll's, so I think to myself, pride or food? (If I bite her, I'll have no food.) So I chose the obvious, I bit her. It was quite a big bite, although it tasted vile!

Then I ran out the front door with Dad running after me. He picked me up by the tail and dangled me over his shoulder.

It's about 10pm. Mum and Pansy are at the hospital and Dad's drunk, hanging from the light. He's already trashed the lounge, he's run upstairs now! He calls me a nutter, he's just run downstairs in a Superman costume, or is it a ballerina? It's hard to tell when you're tied to a coat stand!

I've just tipped the coat stand over and now I am plodding after him with a coat stand on my back.

Oh no! Dad's jumped in through Mrs Sullivas' window! I just got in and at the moment, Dad's keeping away Mrs Sullivas who is defending her cat with an umbrella, only to jump sideways out of the window and land on the pavement!

In fact, I thoroughly enjoyed that, especially raiding her fridge!

Georgia Wells (10)
Manor House School, Devon

THE JUNGLE

One day, I was going to my friend's house when I saw something shiny, like a golden ring. I went to see what it was. I picked it up, but it was a trap and I fell down a hole which was very dark.

I decided to explore and found out that I was in a jungle. It was quite exciting at first, but after a while, I met a tiger. I tried running away from it, but it was too fast, so I had to find a piece of meat.

Instead, I climbed up a tree and tried swinging on a piece of ivy to another tree. Luckily it worked, so I climbed down the tree and went back to the hole that I had fallen down.

I went to see what that shiny thing was, but it was just a chocolate wrapper. I tried climbing up the wall that I hadn't seen before. I climbed up it and I got out of the jungle and went on to my friend's house, up by the bike shop.

Edward Parr (9)
Manor House School, Devon

WEREWOLF VILLAGE

Once upon a time, there were four men and their names were Phil, Paul, Steve and Richard. One night-time, Richard decided to make a potion. When he made it, he gave some to his friends. When they all drank it, they felt fur growing on their bodies and their teeth growing big and sharp. Tails were also growing on them and then they found out that they were werewolves. Everyone else moved out of the village and from then on, the village was called Werewolf Village.

Now that they were wolves, they went into the garden and then they went down into the sewer. In the sewer, there was dirt and mud. They liked it in the sewer.

One day, a brave little girl went down into the sewer and spied on the werewolves. The werewolves caught sight of the little girl. The little girl ran back to her house, like the wind.

In the morning, the little girl went back to the werewolves' hideout. The werewolves spotted the girl again. The girl just stood still. The little girl ran round and round the sewer, then she quickly grabbed the potion, jumped up onto a table and poured it in their open mouths, then they stopped running after the little girl. They started to turn back into humans and so everyone went back into the village and they all lived happily ever after.

Amelia Figgins (8)
Manor House School, Devon

THE WITCH

A boy called Tim was playing in the woods with his friend, Will. They found a house. They guessed it was abandoned.

They approached it slowly and quietly. They went inside. It was dark, but they found a light switch. They went upstairs and looked around and in one room, they saw a witch making a potion. She had green skin with warts. She turned around and saw them! Will ran out of the house, but the witch caught Tim.

Will went back into the house. He went to the same room as before but the witch wasn't there, neither was Tim. Then, Will saw a hatch in the wall. He opened it and fell down a stone slide into a secret lab. He hid behind a spare cauldron and saw the witch lock Tim in a cage. Tim started to shout, 'Help!' Then the witch went to look in a cupboard.

Will ran over and kicked the witch into the cupboard and locked the door. After that he went and freed Tim, but just after he had got him out, the witch burst out of the cupboard and sent a ball of flames hurtling towards them. She missed and the house collapsed on top of her. Tim and Will got home safely, but they never went to the woods again.

James Wells (8)
Manor House School, Devon

THE WITCH

Once upon a time there were two children. They were very happy. Their names were Isobel and Rosie. They lived with their mum and dad in a big house. They had a dog called Spotty. Their dog was a Dalmatian.

At the bottom of their garden they had a spooky shed. They were told never to go in there but one morning, at 6:30, Rosie thought she would go and see inside the shed.

She went outside to the garden. She looked in the shed and just then, a witch appeared. She said, 'I am a good witch. I will give you a wish.' Rosie shivered and said, 'I wish you would go away,' and in a cloud of smoke she disappeared and then Rosie went indoors, but she always kept it a secret.

Rebecca Taylor (8)
Manor House School, Devon

THE HAUNTED MANOR

Once upon a time, I went to a haunted manor. I went inside. The stairs were big. It was very, very cold, it was smelly and I was very spooked out. I went to the kitchen. The light was off and it got even colder. I bumped my head on the wall in the kitchen.

I saw a ghost, it dragged me across the floor. The ghost pressed the button and the stairs came up. I went in. I had no choice because I had no way out because of the dragon. The only way out was the hatch. I jumped up, I ran away and went home.

Timothy Hughes (7)
Manor House School, Devon

THE GHOST WOOD

A little boy was looking for his hat and then he saw something moving in the trees. He looked a bit closer, then it suddenly disappeared, so he just went on looking for his hat. He found his hat and went home.

In the morning, he went back to where he saw something. He went into the wood and kept on walking. Soon he saw a little house and something was moving again, and then it disappeared. He still kept on walking and then he saw another, and another, and another, and then he realised - they were ghosts!

He ran home as fast as he could, then he realised they were friendly. He ran back and the ghost gave him a bun. 'Thank you,' he said and he made friends with the ghosts. He took them to his house and played with them.
'We ghosts call the wood Ghost Wood.'
'That's a good name. I like ghosts,' he said.

The ghosts were very kind to him, so he gave them a bit of chocolate. He loved the ghosts, he played with them every day. He gave them food and water too. The ghosts' best food was ice cream - *yum!*

Annie Parr (8)
Manor House School, Devon

THE TWO WISHES

One sunny morning, William and I were walking on the beach and the sea was rough and the sky was getting darker by the minute. Suddenly thunder roared and the rain poured down and we ran across the sandy beach. We ran for nearly two minutes until we came to a cave. It was a strange looking cave. We ran into the cave to shelter from the rain. William said, 'Let's go on an adventure.'

I said that I didn't think that was such a good idea, but when I looked around, William had gone so I ran after him. I ran for a mile. I saw something green and slimy. I ran on, then I heard someone shouting in the distance. The voice was saying, 'Help! Help!' I ran on thinking it was William.

It was wet and damp. There were strange markings on the walls and it was dark in the cave, but when I looked in my pocket, I found a torch. I switched it on. It was a bit lighter, but the sides were dark and gloomy.

I ran on, struggling with the torch in one hand and running at the same time. When I came to the green and slimy thing, William was not in its arms: a witch was! She said, 'I am a kind witch and I will grant you two wishes.'
I said, 'I wish William was here.' And so he was. Then I said, 'I wish William and I were home.'

Annabel Lumley (7)
Manor House School, Devon

I Went Fishing With My Dad

Once upon a time, I went fishing with my dad at night-time. We went with one of my dad's friends. I was cold and I didn't find any crabs. We didn't get back until ten o'clock at night, then I went to bed.

Michael Arries (8)
Plympton St Maurice Primary School, Devon

THE THREE GHOSTS

Once upon a time there were three ghosts, they scared people away.

It started when the boys were playing in the garden. One of the boys said, 'I know where there are ghosts.' So they went to the castle where there were ghosts playing. One of the boys said, 'Let's go upstairs.' They looked in the bedrooms, then the three ghosts saw them and said, 'Let's scare them!'

The boys saw a ghost playing with a ball, so they ran downstairs into the kitchen. One of the boys said, 'Let's hide in here.' The three ghosts didn't see the boys. One of the boys had a camera and took a picture of a ghost. Then a ghost saw the boys and chased them around the castle. The boys ran out of the castle and never went back.

Richard Carne (8)
Plympton St Maurice Primary School, Devon

THE FAIRY WHO GOT LOST

Once upon a time in a faraway land, there lived a fairy and lots of make-believe animals, like Quadropeck, which has four legs and is a brightly coloured bird, or a Kangodog, which was a dog that could jump like a kangaroo. Everything was just a little bit different.

One day, the fairy went out to get some food for all the animals. On her way back, she tried to take a short cut and she got lost. The trees looked like they had faces and she thought someone was following her. She looked back and she saw nothing. Then she saw a ghost. She flew as fast as she could and she lost him, then she knew where she was. She got home safely and gave the animals their food.

She looked after the animals very well and she cared for them lots. Every Autumn the animals had baby animals. The fairy never took that short cut again.

Nesha Clemens (8)
Plympton St Maurice Primary School, Devon

LOST IN THE JUNGLE

Once upon a time there were two girls. The girls were called Isabelle and Rebecca and they were very good friends.

One day they decided to go out with their friends whose names were Morwenna and Chloe. Morwenna was Isabelle's friend and Chloe was Rebecca's friend. The girls went on their bikes. They got lost, so they went to a man and asked if he could tell them the way back. The man told them how to get back. The girls tried to go the way the man had told them. When the girls stopped, they realised they were more lost, but they weren't lost in the street, they were lost in the *jungle!*
'We're frightened,' said the girls, 'we want to go home,' they continued. Isabelle and Morwenna remembered their friends were only six.

Just then, they heard a sound. The sound was a giant roar! It was a tiger. The girls screamed with fear. The tiger said calmly, 'Don't be afraid. I won't hurt you.' Then he said, 'I will help you.' Suddenly, they heard another roar. 'You girls stay here and I will go,' said the tiger. The tiger knew it was his lost enemy. The girls watched as the tiger approached his enemy. Suddenly, the tiger pounced onto his enemy and that was the end of the fight. The tiger took the girls back across the river to safety.

Isabelle FitzGerald (8)
Plympton St Maurice Primary School, Devon

THE GHOST OF THE MOON

One night, Spike went to bed and wondered why the door was open. He remembered that he had shut the door and thought that it was strange it was now open. He shut the door again and heard a growling noise, it was coming from his wardrobe. He opened the wardrobe door and a ghostly figure came jumping out and said, 'Why did you wake me up?'
'I didn't,' said Spike.
'Oh yes you did,' said the ghostly figure.
'Just who are you?' asked Spike.
'I am the ghost of the moon,' replied the ghostly figure, 'and who are you?'
'I'm Spike,' he said. 'Why are you here anyway?'
'This is my home,' said the ghostly figure.
'No it's not, this is *my* home!' said Spike.
The ghostly figure said, 'Just tell me this, do you know where my family is?'
'I do not know,' said Spike. 'Why, what happened to them?'
'Just over 100 years ago, my parents died in a car accident.'
'Then why are you looking for them?'
'Because I love them,' said the ghostly figure.
'Well, we have a lot in common.'
'Yes we do, don't we?'
'Well, I will see you soon. Goodbye.'

Timothy Hanrahan (8)
Plympton St Maurice Primary School, Devon

THE MAGIC OWL

One night, a white owl was flying when a lightning bolt hit her and gave her magic powers. As she flew on, she saw a pond in the wood. She thought she would have a swim after that shock, so she dived into it.

When she looked in the water, she saw the reflection of a cat coming. She turned round and a big flash came from her eyes and the cat turned to stone. Shea, the owl, was having a great time with her powers, helping hurt animals and saving other creatures in danger. Then, in the morning Shea flew to her nest and went to sleep.

Did I tell you that the pond has a new stone statue of a cat in the middle of it?

Joshua Howarth (7)
Plympton St Maurice Primary School, Devon

CLEVER DAD

One cold, windy night in a small street, there was not a single sound in the air. I suddenly saw a motorbike from nowhere, with a man. He entered my house: I turned all my lights out. Three figures came in, they were as scary as they come. I noticed it was not three figures, they were all attached, as one. I fled in fear. The three-headed person came upstairs and I went through a trapdoor to escape.

Underground, I saw something with pointed teeth and a cape, it was a vampire. I was trapped, there was no way out. Then I saw a shining light, the vampire disappeared. It was my mum and dad's car.

I ran upstairs, but I was too late. There was a troll and a three-headed dog, and then came a zombie. They got my mum and dad, but I saw them put them on their car. Dad snuck off before they played pass-the-car. Suddenly, a man in a cloak appeared, playing a musical pipe. All the monsters vanished. The man in the cloak was my dad. He had read a book on making monsters disappear. Clever Dad.

Matthew Keane (8)
Plympton St Maurice Primary School, Devon

JODIE, THE MAD FOOTBALLER

Jodie loves football. She has a best friend called Charlotte, who likes football as well.

One day, Jodie and Charlotte went on the school field to play football with the boys. Jodie got the ball off the boys. One of the boys went to get it back and Jodie tackled him and he fell over. When he went to get up, he could not stand on his foot and he fell back down. Jodie had broken his ankle, so he was taken to the hospital. The footballers carried on playing and Jodie tackled another boy and broke his leg. Now the boys will not play football with Jodie, the mad footballer, anymore!

Kieran Painter (8)
Plympton St Maurice Primary School, Devon

THOMAS BUILDS A NEW RAILWAY

One day, Thomas decided to build a new railway, so he called all of his friends and asked them if they would help him. They all said yes, so the next day, the building began.

Mavis and Percy brought track from the quarry and started to lay the new track with the help of Cranky the crane, who helped to make a new bridge. Terrence, the tractor, also helped with moving the track to its new place near the local zoo.

Edward, Gordon and Henry got really cross as the troublesome trucks were being naughty and not doing as they were told, which is not unusual as they are always in trouble. It took them five months to finish.

The big day arrived when the new railway would be open. The Fat Controller would be opening it, but first he thanked Thomas and his friends for all their hard work. He was just in time as Bertie and Bulgy pulled up, filled with loads of passengers all eager to visit the new zoo and ride in the new coaches being pulled by Thomas on his new railway line.

David Pryke (8)
Plympton St Maurice Primary School, Devon

SPOOKY

One dark, stormy night, I heard a noise. Suddenly all the doors slammed shut as the wind howled and branches fell from tall trees. People stared out of their windows thinking that someone had cursed our village from the haunted house up on the hill.

People say that headless knights, ghosts, witches, bats, devils and vampires live in the haunted house, but nobody knows. We all know someone lives there. Who is it and what are they? We never know if it would take someone away, or put a curse on the village.

One night there was a scream coming from the house next door. We would not dare to look out of our windows because if it saw us, it would take us too.

The next day, the screaming had stopped. Everyone stepped out of their houses to see who was not there. When everyone was out, my sister's friend Kayleigh was not there. It had taken Kayleigh and it might take another person. Kayleigh was never seen again . . .

Holly Rixon (8)
Plympton St Maurice Primary School, Devon

THE SKELETON

One day I woke up and I saw a skeleton. I decided to make friends with the skeleton. One of my friends ran away. I found his family. The ghost did not go to the family, because they had poison in their bones. My dad let me take him to school.

At school, my teacher made him a desk. During PE, I could not get on the climbing frame, so the skeleton let me climb up his bones. I saw a wire, so I pulled it and the poison came out. I told the skeleton and he started to cry.

The next morning, he had a cold. I brought him a hot drink and a bun. I went to the shop to get him some medicine and when I returned home, he had died. I cried and cried.

Carl Smith (7)
Plympton St Maurice Primary School, Devon

SPOOKY CASTLE

One day, two days before the end of term, Nesha sent out an invitation for six of her friends to go to her house for three weeks. She asked Dane, Jessica, Holly, Morwenna, David and Tejay. Nesha and her friends went to her house. A bit later on, Jessica said, 'Let's go to this really spooky castle so we can play blind man's buff.' Nesha and the others thought that was a great idea, so that night Nesha, Jessica, David, Holly, Tejay, Morwenna and Dane went to this spooky castle.

In this spooky castle there were secrets even Jessica didn't know about. They went to this castle and they were freaked out of their bodies, because they opened the door and they saw zombies, and huge cobwebs with huge spiders in the cobwebs. They walked in and there was a bat. It was huge, a flying fox. All the children just screamed and ran up the slippery, wet, concrete stairs. The zombies chased them. Nesha screamed as loud as she could, *'Run!'*
Jessica picked up a gun and said, 'If you come any closer, you're dead.' But Jessica forgot that you could never kill a zombie and she tried to shoot it. The zombie fell to the ground. Suddenly, there was a great *crash!* The zombie was dead.

Morwenna Summerhill (8)
Plympton St Maurice Primary School, Devon

MY HOLIDAY

On Monday, April 2nd I woke up at about 6:15am. I was excited about going on holiday to Butlins. I couldn't wait to get there, just to go on the Fox Kids play area and the fair rides. It was taking ages for us to leave, but as soon as we did leave in our car, I fell asleep.

I woke up when we were nearly there. I could see Butlins just over the hill. I was so excited! When we go there, I went straight to Fox Kids playhouse and that is where my holiday really began.

Dane Willcocks (8)
Plympton St Maurice Primary School, Devon

A Bear In The Woods

Once upon a time, there lived two people in a house. The people were called Max and Molly, they both hunt for bears. They didn't know there was a bear in the woods.

One day, Max and Molly went out to hunt for bears. Molly saw a bear and told Max. They hid behind a bush because the bear nearly saw them. Then the bear came round the bush and saw Max and Molly. Molly turned around and saw the bear and she screamed, then Max turned around and they both screamed very loudly and ran into their house. They both forgot to shut the door, so they both quickly shut the door so that the bear did not get them.

The bear tried to climb up to the roof to get down the chimney, but he fell onto a log fire. The bear flew up the chimney and back down, landing on a pile of stinging nettles.

He tried another plan but it didn't work because he went through a window, Max punched him and the bear fell on the floor and hurt him. The bear said, 'Oh no.' The bear tried to break the door down but he couldn't, so he just went back home and he never bothered Max and Molly ever again, and I am not joking.

Jessica Willcocks (8)
Plympton St Maurice Primary School, Devon

THE HORROR HOTEL

At last we had reached the Hollywood Hotel. As we queued to get a room, I saw a statue of an owl, his yellow eyes glared at me. I shook. Everything was covered in a thick layer of dust. Cobwebs covered the ceiling and the tattered remains of tall white pillars stood everywhere.

Our room was on the top floor, in the longest corridor right at the back of the hotel. The lady at the desk gave us the keys and said, 'Please go to the boiler room and use the service elevator, the main lift is out of order.'

As we entered the boiler room we could hear the hissing pipes spitting out water from their cracks. The last words we heard were, 'Enjoy your ride!' the lift doors slammed shut and we travelled up five storeys more than we should have. We hung there. The lift doors opened wide, revealing to us the bare brick walls at the top of the hotel. The cable suddenly split and we dropped; it seemed to go at sixty miles per hour. We hit the ground!

If you ever visit the Hollywood Hotel, I suggest you take the stairs.

Joanna Lewis (9)
Plympton St Maurice Primary School, Devon

WHAT WAS IT?

Once day in space, a rather small planet called Pluto was *crashing down to Earth,* when a Gem exploded out of Pluto and Pluto was gone. It had exploded because of the Gem's powers. A spaceman in a rocket succeeded in catching the Gem that exploded out of Pluto.

The spaceman was taking it back to Earth, when it just started to glow and then it turned red. The spaceman touched it and it burned his hand. Arrrghhhh! Then it melted the ship and then the Earth. It was all over. No one was alive but the spaceman and the Gem, as he watched the blue goo pour out of it.

What was it?

Chris Tomlinson (9)
Plympton St Maurice Primary School, Devon

THE LOST PURSE

In a very large town lived an old lady called Mrs Honey. She was given this name because she loves honey. One day when Mrs Honey went for a walk, she dropped her purse and walked along.

After a while, a little girl came and saw the purple purse lying on the filthy floor. She quickly picked it up and kept on walking.

When the little old lady got home and looked in her black bag she was shocked her purse had disappeared. The lady looked everywhere around the house and still there was no sight of the little purple purse.

The little girl was trying to find who the purse belonged to. The poor girl had been looking all day long and then it turned afternoon. She had nothing to eat, so she went hungry. There was only one door left that she had forgotten to do, number 60. She was so scared, she shivered.

Suddenly, she knocked on the door with a loud *bang*. An old lady opened it and croaked, 'Yes, can I help you?'
'Is this your purse?'
'Yes, thank you very much.'

So this is what you do, you always give things back.

Latesha Claffey (9)
Plympton St Maurice Primary School, Devon

THE SHADOW ON THE FARM

Ben, Jo and Jon were staying at their grandparents' big, old farmhouse in the middle of nowhere. They liked playing around the barns where the animals were kept, but they were afraid of Joseph, the mean-looking farmhand. He was cruel to the animals and scowled and shouted at the children.

One night, they were woken by a loud crash of thunder and the shutters banging on the windows. Then they heard footsteps running down the stairs and out of the front door. They looked out across the yard and saw a faint shadow of a boy entering the barn where Joseph slept. There was a loud scream. They saw Joseph staggering with the shadow towards the well. Then there was silence and only the shadow was seen moving back towards the house. Once again they heard footsteps, followed by the bang of the attic door closing.

They told their grandfather in the morning what they had seen and he told them that years ago, a young farmhand had mysteriously disappeared. They all went out to the well and at the bottom lay Joseph. Who killed him?

Bradley Ball (9)
Plympton St Maurice Primary School, Devon

LOST IN THE WOODS

One day, Mandy went into the woods to have a picnic. She sat by the stream so after she'd finished, she could have a swim.

Because Mandy was so busy skipping along the path looking at all the pretty flowers, she went the wrong way. Before Mandy knew it, she was in the middle of the woods, lost and all on her own. The sun had set and it was getting darker and darker. Mandy was very scared and didn't know what to do, so she walked and walked.

It was very, very dark and Mandy was cold. When she saw a cabin hiding behind some trees, she went up to it and opened the door. It creaked loudly and some bats flew out of the door. Mandy felt something at her leg, she looked down and saw two eyes looking back at her. It was Jack, the wolf. Behind Jack was an ugly, old witch called Charlotte.

Mandy jumped and they chased her up the stairs to Josh, the ghost. Mandy turned around, pushed past Charlotte and ran into the kitchen. On the floor were four dead bodies. Mandy screamed and ran her fastest home, and never went back again.

Charlotte Vosper (9)
Plympton St Maurice Primary School, Devon

THE HAUNTING

A long time ago, there lived a man called Frederic. He lived in a big house on a hill. Every time people came to the house, he would invite them in. When inside, they had to stay there. He would lock all the doors and scare them. He would turn into a wolf and kill a man by ripping him in two. But one day, the guests all pushed Frederic in the cupboard and no one went back to the house on the hill.

Bradley Warren (8)
Plympton St Maurice Primary School, Devon

WHERE'S FROSTIE?

One day, the removal van came to move Alice and her family to a new house. Alice was excited because she had a big room. Alice put Frostie, the cat, in his cat box. Frostie wasn't happy, he didn't like it in the box.

When they arrived, they brought in furniture, unpacked and made beds. Alice was having a great time. Alice let Frostie out of his box. He was free. Frostie ran somewhere. Alice and her family searched around the house. They looked high and low, nobody found him.

Alice was tired, so she went to look for the box with her pyjamas inside. She opened the box and out jumped Frostie.

Leah Cragg (9)
Plympton St Maurice Primary School, Devon

The Ghost!

One stormy night, there were two boys who lived in a haunted mansion, but they were on their own because their parents had died and they had no friends or relatives. They had lived there for eleven years and they were miserable. Their names were Zack and Jack. Zack was fifteen and Jack was fourteen.

One night Zack heard a whooshing sound. He opened the door slightly and he saw a big ghost. It was huge and it was as white as a piece of A4 plain paper. Zack snuck past the ghost and went into Jack's room and told him about the ghost.

At first, Jack didn't believe Zack, but the next night they both saw it. A while later, they saw a little boy put the ghost costume on. The next night, they both saw the ghost together and they pulled the costume off and saw the little boy. They asked the boy if he wanted to live with them and he said 'Yes please!'

Andrew Endean (9)
Plympton St Maurice Primary School, Devon

A Spook Of A Trip

It was a beautiful day as Charlie and Tim set off on their camping expedition to the moors. They found a lovely place to camp by next to what they thought was a nice, quiet wood. Working out how to put their tent up, the two boys decided to enter the woods.

Loud groans echoed throughout the woods. The boys turned white. Charlie whispered, 'What's that white thing over there?'
'Oh no, it's a ghost.' Tim shook.
Suddenly, the spooky thing turned around. 'Why are you in my woods?' he bellowed at the frozen figures.
'We came to get our ball,' the boys replied.
With that, the ghost hurled the ball over their heads and into the hands of a huge monster creeping up on them.
'Please can we have our ball back?'
He chucked the ball at them, knocking them both over. They ran back to their camp.

Thomas Brown (9)
Plympton St Maurice Primary School, Devon

MAD MEN

One night, a lady called Martha was watching the 6 o'clock news. There were reports on people dying. Martha was scared, so she decided to leave New York. She sprinted downstairs and got into her car without locking the door.

She went full speed down the motorway. Suddenly, a red car started following her. Then a loud crash sounded on the roof. It was a mad chainsaw man trying to cut through the roof. Martha opened the sunroof and it fell off and hit the side of a lorry.

As she turned the bend, she realised the red car wasn't trying to harm her, but was trying to warn her about the made axe man in the back of her car.

Harry Sherwin (9)
Plympton St Maurice Primary School, Devon

GHOST IN THE LOFT!

Ben lived in a flat with his mum and brother. Ben's flat was very untidy because his mum never tidied up.

On a very cold winter's day, Ben's mum heard loud noises coming from the loft. The next day, Ben wanted to play in the park with his friends, but his football boots were in the loft. He quickly opened the hatch, pulled down the ladder then climbed up to the loft. When he got there, he saw his football boots in the air. Then something said, 'I am a ghost.'
Ben said, 'Do you want to play football with me?'
'Yes,' said the ghost, so they played for ages until Ben's mum said, 'What are you doing? Your friends are waiting for you. Come on.'
'I'm sorry, I have to go now. Can I have back my boots please?'

Five minutes later.
'Ben, dinner's ready.'
'Ow, stop kicking the ball at me. Ow!'
Then one of Ben's friends who was angry with Ben, went to hit him, until . . . the ghost grabbed Ben and threw him in the air, out of the way. From then on, Ben let the ghost use his football boots whenever he wanted and the ghost looked after Ben.

Emily Pope (9)
Plympton St Maurice Primary School, Devon

CANDY MAN

One scary night some boys were telling ghost stories and one boy had a mirror. He said 'Candy Man' three times, then a man with a hook appeared. He pulled their livers out and ate them and when he was finished, he went off to kill some more people.

He saw a policeman. He nicked his clothes and then he got a 20 inch knife and sliced his head off. Then he saw a cat, so he gave it a shave. Then it became morning, so Candy Man disappeared.

Then day went and it was dark again. *Eek, eek.* He heard a guinea pig, so he cut its head off and turned it into a sausage. He still had police clothes on and an old lady thought he was a policeman, so he cut her into five pieces. Anyone that got in his way, he shredded them.

There was this other man who wanted to take over the world, so he got mad. His name was Jeepers Creepers, he wanted a match with Candy Man. Jeepers Creepers used a 30 inch axe and sliced Candy Man into two pieces and then stabbed anyone that was there.

Thomas Downs (9)
Plympton St Maurice Primary School, Devon

A Viking Ring

One fine summer's day I was going to the beach in Wembury. I went out onto the golden sand by the blue seawater. I was digging a hole, when there was a glint of light. It was a ring. I picked it up carefully. I looked round the silver edge, it said, 'Whoever reads these words will get a Viking day out.'

A Viking suddenly appeared. He said, 'What shall we go on first?'
'Boating.'
He gave a wave, a boat came to the shore. It had lots of oars and a dragon's head on the front. On deck, we started to row. Suddenly, a rock was flying towards us. *Bang!* We were sinking.

I awoke; part of a boat and the ring lay beside me.

Joshua Egan (9)
Plympton St Maurice Primary School, Devon

SOUTH PARK COMES ALIVE

One day, Alex was watching South Park and it was a Hallowe'en special. He was so excited, until his mum came in. 'I'm going out. I don't want you to watch this,' his mum said. She took the batteries out of the controller and put them in her handbag and went.

He got his dad's toolbox and took out what looked like a battery. It went in the remote perfectly. He put on South Park. Suddenly, there was a big flash and there, right in front of him, were Stan, Kyle, Cartman and Kenny.

Cartman said, 'Dude, I think we're in a portal.'
'Shut up, fat boy,' said Stan.
Kenny said, 'Mrppphm, mrppphm,' under his coat.
'Ha, ha,' laughed Stan, Kyle and Kenny.

They all went out trick-or-treating. All of a sudden, Kenny went missing. A character from South Park appeared, holding Kenny's head. 'Oh my God, you killed Kenny,' said Stan.

They all went back to Alex's house. 'Quick, press rewind,' said Kyle. 'See ya.' The big flash again. They all disappeared.

Alex Neville (9)
Plympton St Maurice Primary School, Devon

GHOST

Once upon a time, a long way from here, there was a boy called Tom. One day, Tom was playing out in his back garden. He was lying down next to his next-door neighbour's fence. Suddenly, this head popped over the gate. The man said, 'Hello Tom.'
'How do you know my name?' Tom said.

The man said, 'Follow me, Tom.' Suddenly, the man grabbed Tom. Then Tom turned around. Somebody stabbed the man with a sword, but there was no one there, so Tom went home.

Shawn Norton (9)
Plympton St Maurice Primary School, Devon

THE SECRET

Chapter 1

My name is Tobias, a freak of nature, one of a kind. I won't tell you my last name. I can't tell you my last name, or the name of my city where I live. I am a normal kid. I can't even tell you my identity. My friend Morphed, had a secret too.

Chapter 2

On the next day, a new boy came into school. The boy had a secret too. One day, a fireman came into school to talk to us.

Chapter 3

Suddenly, the two mates changed their minds. The boy turned into an eagle and the girl turned into a lobster. They couldn't go back to class like this. Or could they?

Jordan Powlesland (8)
Plympton St Maurice Primary School, Devon

CHASED

I am a wolf. I live in North America. I live in a big pack of wolves and I eat rabbits and weasels.

One day, I had a litter of cubs. Some hunters were coming and they took three of my cubs. I chased after them, but they got away. I picked up the scent of my cubs and the trail took me to a log house.

I looked through the window and saw my cubs, so I dug under the log house to get them. I was just about to get out, but the hunters came in. I howled and all of the other wolves came and attacked the hunters. I was very glad to get my cubs back.

Craig Hunkin (10)
Werrington Primary School, Cornwall

THE SCORPION

Hello, I am a scorpion and I'm going to tell you a story.

One day, I woke up in my hole and heard a lot of banging. I stuck my head out of the hole and I saw lots of men cutting down trees. A tree nearly squashed me and I jumped out of the way. Then I ran for it. I ran and ran until I reached the town.

A man nearly stepped on me, so I stung him and ran across the road. I popped a car tyre as well, because it nearly ran me over.

I kept on running down the street until I met another man. He picked me up with some gloves and took me all the way back to the forest, and somehow, all the people had gone, so I scurried into my hole and went to sleep again.

Bob Carr (10)
Werrington Primary School, Cornwall

EAGLE OWL

One day I was flying above the woods, when I saw a river swimming with fish. I swooped down and I was about to grab a fish when I heard a gunshot, so I flew away. I carried on flying until I saw them, so I flew down into a tree and hid.

Eventually they shot again and my cousin, the horned owl, came falling out of the sky. I flew away. Six bullets came after me, but I got away. From then on, I watched my every move. I went to find the hunters' home.

Just when the sun was setting, I found their home. I looked in the window and saw my mother, I tried to get in, but I couldn't. I started to worry, but then I thought of a plan. I went to find my twin. When I found him, I told him my plan and we went back to the hunters' home. This time, we opened the door, my twin flew in and came out again with the hunters chasing him. I flew in and opened all the cages and we all flew out and the hunters never came back.

Jack Basford (9)
Werrington Primary School, Cornwall

SNAKE

I'm Hiss, and I'm a snake. I live in the jungle. I haven't got many friends, only a few. One day, I fell into a trap and got caught and I got taken in a cage. I was put into another cage and then I realised where I was when people started to walk by. I was in a zoo.

I started to panic, then I saw a person, very small. The person had a stone and he threw it at the glass cage. It cracked. The person kept doing it and doing it until the glass broke altogether.

I slithered out as quickly as I could. I was out at last, only a few minutes in there scares me because I live so close to a zoo. I have to beware of traps like that one. I will go back now because I'm hungry and want to get back to my friends.

I slithered back, managing not to get stepped on by a human. I will go and tell Slith first about my journey, and then Slip, and I will tell all my friends. I am really hungry now.

Alice Warring (10)
Werrington Primary School, Cornwall

TRAPPED

As I prowled through the jungle looking for food, I could smell a strange smell. It was like the jungle was covered in this unfamiliar stink. I saw something moving in the foliage of the tree. I jumped and pounced. Unfortunately, I didn't catch the creature. Hang on, what was that? I jumped on it and suddenly, I was strung up in a net.

I tried to get out but I couldn't. Men came and they were saying something. All I wanted was to get out. Their strange voices irritated me. I started to growl and snarl, like a proper tiger should do. They just made laughing gestures. One of the men put out his dark hand, but I bit it.

I couldn't stand it. Here I was, stuck in the net and they were just laughing. The tanned man's hand was bleeding very badly.

The other man released me finally. As I clambered out, I gave one last growl and ran off. Good job Jala, I thought. I'm the best tiger in India.

Abigail Williams (11)
Werrington Primary School, Cornwall

THE SECRET CAVE

I was at the beach one day when I saw a cave. I ran inside and there was lots of treasure, so I picked some up. Suddenly, a ghost came out from nowhere and started to chase me. I ran into a tunnel, but the ghost kept on chasing me so I kept on running.

Suddenly, I came to a dead end. I was very frightened. All these other ghosts appeared. Then my mum came running down the tunnel and scared the ghosts off. We ran out as quickly as we could. I was pleased to see my mum. She said I was not to go off on my own again.

Ben Jenkin (9)
Werrington Primary School, Cornwall

SPECIAL DELIVERY

Just before the baby was born . . .

Dear Diary,

I'm sad. This baby is going to take over my life and my room. Mum and Dad pushed my bed into the corner and packed away all my toys to make room for the baby's new things. There was so much baby stuff you could hardly move.

I was hoping the baby would be a boy so we could interact with each other. I felt quite excited and I was wondering what it was going to be like. I also hoped that it would be healthy. Would my mum love me as much, or would the baby become her favourite?

After the baby was born . . .

I didn't like the baby at first because it had and angry little face and it cried a lot. I was pleased it was a boy and he was healthy. Mum even let me name him. His name is Vegita, but I call him Geta for short.

I help feed him and put his clothes on. He has tiny little hands and feet and he's very cute. When he sees me he makes little gurgling sounds. I think I might share my toys with him after all, because it's nice to have a brother as a friend.

Michael Hall (10)
West Hill Primary School, Devon

MR MOLE AND MR SQUIRREL

One morning, Mr Mole dug a big hole for a trap for Mr Squirrel to come along and fall in. Mr Mole waited and waited until he got fed up, so he went over to the hole that he had dug to see if Mr Squirrel had fallen in, but he wasn't in the hole. He wondered where Mr Squirrel was. Suddenly from nowhere, Mr Squirrel came down from the tree and pushed Mr Mole in.

'Golly gosh!' shrieked Mole, who got up and brushed himself down. 'Who was that?' asked Mole. When Mole found out it was Mr Squirrel he was very surprised. 'Give me a hand up, will you?' said Mole.
But Mr Squirrel just stared.

'There's lots of nuts down here,' exclaimed Mole. As nuts were Mr Squirrel's favourite, he jumped in but just then Mr Mole clambered over Mr Squirrel's head and escaped with a cheeky smile on his face.

Alistair Slade (11)
West Hill Primary School, Devon

BLEAK HOUSE

I felt worried when my mum and dad died and I thought that Charley might die, and I would have to look after baby Emma and we would not have enough money to buy any food. I sometimes feel abandoned by my family. I know Charley has to work, but I miss her so much and I think Emma does too. We both feel so happy when Charley gets home. I have a glimpse of pleasure in my life when I am with Charley. She makes me so happy. Sometimes I pray at night and ask God for Charley, Emma and I to live forever and for it to all work out. I pray at night in the candlelight, before I go to bed.

Charley is my sister, but she acts like my mum. She is very good to me and I am grateful to her. Charley helps me not to miss my mum and dad now that they have died. I am so glad to have Charley for a sister. I do really love her very much, just as I love my little baby Emma, she is very sweet too.

Aimée Snell (10)
West Hill Primary School, Devon

TRAPPED

It was coming all along. We didn't get hurt, well, not on the outside.

I'm Pete. Jamie will be here in a minute. Ah, here he is now. Let's go to the library now.
'Come on Jamie, to the fairy tale section.'
'Little Red Riding Hood's here, let's get reading,' I told Jamie.
'OK,' Jamie said quietly.

When I got to the fourth page, something funny started to happen. We started to get sucked into the book. We couldn't do anything about it, we just went with the flow . . .

A girl with a red cloak was standing outside a house. It was Little Red Riding Hood! 'Who are you?' she said.
'We're Jamie and Pete. We got sucked into your book!'
'Don't worry, it always happens.'
'Phew,' said Jamie, 'how do we get out?'
'You can't,' she snarled.
'The wolf!' we shouted. We ran for our lives. What should we do, I thought.

The wolf gained on us. He grabbed us by the legs. Finally, he bit us. Now, we're in Heaven. We had a happy life, but the ending was a bit sad. I warn you to never go near the Little Red Riding Hood book, otherwise you'll regret it!

Michael Rose (11)
West Hill Primary School, Devon

THE RUBY OF ITARTAS

Josephina sat on the boat which swayed to and fro. They were on their way to the Cairo Museum to investigate the artefacts. They finally were there and walked in the museum. Josephina looked at a crown and necklace that looked oddly familiar.

Her toes tingled, a shiver went down her spine, her eyes burned. She closed them. Then voices died away, everything was quiet.

'Cleopatra, Your Highness.' She opened her eyes quickly to the warm voice. 'Have you seen the Ruby of Itartus?' he asked in a worried tone.
'No,' spoke Josephina. Josephina suddenly had a wave of guilt rush over her.

She was wearing the crown she had seen, and a long white dress. In her pocket, something was weighing her down. She looked in her pocket. It was the Ruby of Itartus.

Just then, the Pharaoh came around the corner and the Ruby of Itartus fell out of Jospehina's pocket. *'You!'* thundered the Pharaoh. 'Take her to the snakes!'

She was shoved into the room. Snakes came closer, she tripped and fell down and down and *thump,* she landed on the floor in her own time, 2002, still with the Ruby of Itartus in her hand.

April Down (11)
West Hill Primary School, Devon

TELL ME

My name is Philip. I'm a doctor. One day, something strange happened to me...

Knock, knock. I heard someone knocking on my door. I went over. Through my doorway fell a pilot. He looked ill; being a doctor, I knew exactly what to do. I bathed him and gave him fresh clothes. When he'd dressed, I said to him, 'Tell me.'

'A long time ago, I was flying over the Bermuda Triangle. As I neared the centre of the triangle, it grew foggy. Suddenly, out of the fog came a water spout. It engulfed and dragged me down. I tried to escape, but it was useless. Soon, I was lying on the bottom of the sea. Invisible hands guided me to a chamber. All the while, I was growing short of air. This was too much; I struggled free and swam. I don't know how I managed it, but I reached the surface.

'Incredible tale, almost unbelievable,' I mused, with my back to him. When I turned round, he had vanished...

There you are, my tale. And if you don't believe me, drop in some day and I shall show you the uniform he left behind.

Elinor Puttick (11)
West Hill Primary School, Devon

A Hedgehog, A Rat And A Concrete Mixer

One day, a rat fell in a concrete mixer at a building site. He tried to climb out, but it was spinning too fast, so he kept falling back in. He was just about to give up, when a hedgehog appeared at the rim above the rat's head.

'Mr Hedgehog,' said the rat, with a sneaky idea in mind. 'Would you like to come down here with me? You see, I've been asked by the builders to stay here and squeak when the concrete starts to go hard.'

'What's so good about that?' replied the hedgehog.

'Well,' said the rat, 'I get paid a block of cheese every ten minutes, which means you will probably get a snail every ten minutes!'

Without waiting a second longer, the hedgehog jumped straight down into the concrete mixer. Unfortunately though, the sly little rat jumped, landed on the hedgehog's spikes which bent, then straightened out again, throwing the lying rat to safety on dry land.

'Bye,' chuckled the rat as he scampered away from the building site in the bright sunshine, leaving the hedgehog squeaking for help in the concrete mixer.

Billy Hesmondhalgh (11)
West Hill Primary School, Devon

CHANGES

You won't understand this - even I don't. I never have. Time and again I've wished they hadn't come. Nobody could stop them. They were like people from a film, but this was real.

Debt collectors came, taking belongings, memories and Dad. Dad, an uncut mop of oily black hair, a law-breaker, taking part in money-wasting schemes. Even now, with it all behind us, it's inexplicable. That fateful day, losing everything, will stick in my mind for eternity.

We took the measly amount left to a one-bedroomed flat with unusable, greasy kitchen, bathroom and lounge, desperately needing refurbishment. Not home how did Mum cope?

My back constantly aches from sleeping on the floor and my feet froze there. Mum tried to be cheerful, not succeeding. Oliver - thin and weary, my attempt at help failed.

Visiting Dad was a scarce and downhearted experience. Visiting day - Wednesday - I imagined him waiting. No point in wasted tears, he was to blame.

Mum changed. Smoked, drank. She didn't clean. Lisa's asthma worsened and she was hospitalised, but survived.

An ugly environment for a child - maybe I'm a moaner, but I think you'll agree.

Katie Light (10)
West Hill Primary School, Devon

THE ALLIGATOR, THE SNAKE AND THE QUICKSAND

The alligator was walking through the jungle, when he saw a snake stuck in some sticky quicksand. The snake saw the alligator at the same moment. 'Will you help me?' cried the snake, 'I have five children at home and they need me, so please will you help?'
Well, that wasn't true, just a cover story to get him out.
'Wrap some of your body around my tail and I'll pull you out,' the alligator said, coolly.
So the snake wrapped himself around the alligator's tail and the alligator pulled. He pulled so hard that he turned red instead of green.

Suddenly, the snake was free and because the alligator was so happy, he did a somersault and landed in the quicksand. 'Oh no, help me snake,' wailed the alligator.
'No. You shouldn't have helped me. You know my reputation,' and he sauntered off into the bushes.

The moral of this story is: be certain of what you are doing.

Kathryn Rowles (10)
West Hill Primary School, Devon

THE CROCODILE AND THE ANTELOPE

There was once a crocodile who was starving, as he hadn't had anything to eat for weeks on end. He was resting in his dark, gloomy swamp, when an antelope appeared. 'Is the plant life in there good?' asked the antelope naturally.

Well, the crocodile knew that all the plants had died long before, but he thought of a clever plan to get him some food. 'Yes, it has grown tremendously in the last year,' he replied.
'Would I be allowed to try some?' questioned the antelope again.
'Why yes, of course,' answered the crocodile.

With that, the antelope trudged into the mess, but at that, the crocodile sprang onto the antelope's back and hauled it under the surface. The crocodile held it there until it drowned. Then he dragged the poor, foolish antelope to the bottom of the swamp and put him under a log to decay. At last the crocodile had got something to eat. What a crafty croc!

Samuel Bowker (10)
West Hill Primary School, Devon

WHERE I BELONG

India's my home. Father's died, Mother's in charge. She's leaving our home and sending me to England. She thinks she can take memories away, but she can't! Memories are mine. It won't be my home, never.

She packed my clothes. She's going to Africa - I'm going to England. My board's paid. I'm going to boarding school. Never been to school. On a ship I'm going.

I'm in England, I'm at school. They showed me my room. I lay there dreaming. Didn't go for dinner.

Days later, I knew it was a bad thing moving here. Food was sloppy, I'm a slave, I'm running away!

No chance. Mrs Twitchard called me into her office. She told heart-shattering news - mother's died. I was to get a black dress and become a slave. I had only memories. Trapped I was, no luxuries.

I'm going to change, change life for everyone. I'll become a teacher. I'll change school. An exam I'm to take. It churned my stomach . . . I passed. My ambitions were complete when my students' dreams came true. They thanked me . . . I changed school. Now time to return to India, back where I belong, set free of the trap, the burden.

Melissa Crombie (11)
West Hill Primary School, Devon

LITTLE YELLOW RIDING HOOD

'Oh, darling daughter of mine!'
'Yes, Mum.'
'Remember Granny still wants to see you, although she is ill.'
'Yes, Mum.'
'Oh, Yellow Riding Hood?'
'Yes, Mum!'
'Be good?'
'Yes, Mum.'

Once upon a time, there was a girl called Yellow Riding Hood. She lived with her mother on the edge of a forest. She was walking along when ... 'Yo lil' girl!'
She spun around and saw a wolf. 'I'm off to my gran's house,' said Yellow Riding Hood.
'Lickin', wickin', eatin' da chicken! That path is quicker,' said the wolf. Yellow Riding Hood set off.
'Or was it longer?' he whispered.

Soon, Yellow Riding Hood arrived. She opened the door and went in.
'Hi Gran, what big eyes you have,' said the girl.
'Ain't they wicked!' replied the wolf, who had bundled Granny in the cupboard.
'What big teeth you have,' said Yellow Riding Hood.
'They're to eat you with, my dear.'

Smack! Grandma had chopped her way out of the cupboard and hit the wolf. 'Hi Gran,' said Yellow Riding Hood.
'Ready for your martial arts lesson?' said the old woman.
'Yes, Gran,' replied Yellow Riding Hood.

Peter Cowan (11)
West Hill Primary School, Devon

CHANGES

Louise, Sara and Amy are triplets and do everything together. They were exploring an old ruin on Dartmoor and discovered a wonderful den. 'Oh, wow!' exclaimed Sara, 'Look what I've found!'

Amy and Louise rushed over shouting. They all peered down a dark hole. Everyone jumped down and Amy found a switch. She pressed it and a dim light flickered on.

'Wow!' they all chorused. They saw an entrance to a maze, as high as the room. Cautiously, they edged over to it. a few minutes later, they came across a room with shelves, swings, beds and a rope ladder, not forgetting the table.

It took them weeks to decorate it with colours they all agreed on, despite being triplets. When they eventually finished, it looked stunning. Their mother called them one day and told them to go and stay with their grandma. None of them wanted to go, but Mother insisted.

They spent four weeks at their grandma's. It seemed like four years! When they came back, they ran to their bedroom upstairs, opened the door and . . . the whole room had changed. It was painted their worst colours. They sat down and thought, things *do* change, and this is their day.

Camilla Russell (10)
West Hill Primary School, Devon

NIGHTMARE!

'Goodnight, Mum!' I shouted as I walked up the wooden stairs to my room. 'See you tomorrow.' I climbed into my cosy bed, exhausted, drifting to sleep. But that was when it happened . . . the nightmare.

I woke up after a terrible dream, the worst. It was as though I was being sucked in, pulled down, made to believe the truth . . .

I looked around me, I was sitting on the dirt of the ground. Everybody around me was carrying goods, or sweeping the dusty ground, doing whatever these rulers told them . . . the Vikings. 'Get up and do your work,' said a soldier. Tears rolling down my face, I got up. Isn't this just me imagining things, a dream?

I woke in the morning thinking I was in my own bed, but I realised. I looked at the bed, nothing but mud, then looked out at the fields. Men and women working.

I was trapped in the past, or maybe my life in the 21st century was a wish, a simple dream.

Rebecca James (11)
West Hill Primary School, Devon

THE THREE FROGS

Once upon a time, there were three frogs. They lived in a place of wonder. It was called The Furry Forest Of Beach Town.

There was once a dragonfly who was looking for somewhere to rest as he had to head for the west. There were three lily pads in a row on the calm pond. He went and sat on the first one. 'This one's too slimy and lumpy,' the dragonfly said. He tried and tried, but he was too uncomfortable, so he went to the next lily pad. It was all cold and horrid, so he went to the next one. This lily pad was fine. What he did not notice was the frogs were swimming back.

'Someone's been sleeping in my bed,' said the daddy frog.
'Someone's been sleeping in my bed,' said the mummy frog.
'Someone's *in* my bed,' shouted the baby frog and woke the dragonfly up.
'I'm sorry,' said the dragonfly and flew off, heading west.

Amelia Colwill (10)
West Hill Primary School, Devon

THE TALE OF TWO MICE

The large hole loomed nearer and nearer as the mice skated frantically across the floor with the enemy on their tails. Back in the safety of their lair, they turned to each other and said, 'We've beaten that cat, once and for all!'

They removed their clothes and threw them across the floor. Suddenly, the phone rang. 'Not another call for help,' said one mouse to the other, and sure enough, they were needed. Fellow mice were in danger. Kitted up in goggles, capes and boots, they ventured out into the unknown once again, to save a fellow mouce. The two mice against the world, to open the fridge door and to free a mouse friend who was trapped inside, freezing to death.

'This is a race against time,' said one of the mice. Tails tugging, they pulled the door open and the mouse was sitting on a mound of cheese, looking very smug. Now he was rescued, everyone was well fed on the cheese. The two mice were pleased with their rescue, so they strolled back to the office, ready for another call.

Mercedes Pemberton-Finch (11)
West Hill Primary School, Devon

KENSINGTON'S VASE

It was a bank holiday and Mongoose and Kezzie went youth hostelling. But while they were staying, they had started to find bones everywhere.

One night, they heard crying from under the bed.
'Do you think it is . . ?' Mongoose asked.
'No,' said Kezzie, quickly.
They decided to look under the bed at the same time and as they did, they saw a weird shadow. Kezzie and Mongoose jumped back.
'What's your name?' asked Mongoose.
'Kensington,' he replied.

It turned out they had met a ghost. He told them how he got there and this is what he said.

'It was about 110 years ago. I was a servant in my master's house. He was rich and wealthy. He once bought this great Chinese vase. He asked me to carry it to h is bedroom. It must have been expensive, because he ordered two men to help me with it up the stairs. But I slipped and the vase broke. The next thing I knew was that my master was so angry with me, he was stabbing me in the heart.'

The next morning, Mongoose and Kezzie left, feeling very guilty about leaving Kensington there.

Joseph Tomlins (11)
West Hill Primary School, Devon

The Scream

It was a chilly day as Chloe walked along the moors. Ben, her pet dog, had been missing for three days and she was starting to worry about him. She missed his cuddles and his wet nose on her cheek. Now, it was four o'clock and cold. The weather forecast was for snow and she desperately wanted to find him before he froze.

Just then, Chloe stopped as she heard the most terrible, bloodcurdling scream, which sounded just like a girl. Ben hurtled towards her, a cut across his back, which looked like a person had made it! Whimpering loudly, he led her to a pit in which lay an injured girl, no older than Chloe herself.

It looked like Ben had tried to help, thinking it was Chloe, but had failed. Chloe, who as stronger, pulled her out. She took off her coat and wrapped it around the girl who was too scared to speak.

The hospital soon found the injured girl's parents, who were sick with worry, and told them that the girl was just suffering with shock and bruises. Chloe's parents were phoned and soon came to take her and a shivering Ben home.

Louise Adamson (10)
Whitstone Primary School, Devon

THE SHADOW

It was a dark, gloomy night. The moon was full. Three children dared to go back to school that night. They crept up to the gate, the school was in darkness. They scuttled to the nearest classroom. A light appeared out of the darkness and a shapeless shadow formed in that light. Footsteps shook the floor as something grew nearer. The children hid themselves as the shape came closer, then there was a thunder-shocking footstep, knocking the children off balance. The children scrambled to their feet and scuttled to their classroom. One tried the lights, they flickered and went out. Another pulled out a torch, the light shone through the thick, dark air.

There was a thud on the roof. The children shook, and the door swung open. Smoke seeped into the classroom. The shadow came even closer. At first, the children froze, then seeing what was approaching, terrified, they screamed. They realised the fire exit was their only escape. In a mad panic they tried to get it open. One felt something touch his shoulder. Shocked, he pushed forward, forcing open the door. They all fell out, but still the shadow followed. Where would they run to next?

Ben Roberts & Thomas Gerry (11)
Whitstone Primary School, Devon

THE HAND

It was a cold, rainy night. As a happily married couple were driving home, they saw a deer on the road. The man swerved and the car crashed into a tree. His wife smacked into the dashboard with a deafening sound and her hand smashed through the windscreen. The man's chest hit violently against the steering wheel. A passer-by saw them and phoned 999, they were rushed to hospital.

The woman died after an operation, but the man lived. He missed her so much and wanted something to remember her by.

So the night that she was buried, he crept down to the churchyard and searched for her grave, took out a spade and dug. Then he wrenched open her coffin and stared gloomily at her. As he glanced down at her body, he saw her hand. It was almost ripped off, only behind held on by a few veins.

He tore it off and as he headed back to the gates, they seemed to get further away. Suddenly, the other hand shot out of the grave and grabbed him, pulled him into her grave and he was never seen or heard of again!

Nicholas Coleing (11)
Whitstone Primary School, Devon

ELISE

Bang! Elise's new school bag banged against the wall of the old railway tunnel. Panting, her younger sister Jane stopped behind her. 'Oh no!' groaned Elise, 'I forgot it.'
'Well go and get it back, you can't go home without it,' said Jane.

Elise dashed back along the tunnel. When she arrived back at school, she ran straight to her classroom. *Whoosh!* Something moved, quick as a knife through shadows and into the next classroom. Elise ran into the class, grabbed her pen from her drawer, then suddenly a torch flashed in the corridor. Elise felt the hairs on the back of her neck stiffen. She looked for somewhere to hide, then the thing came into the classroom. Elise looked for somewhere to escape. All she saw was a window and without any hesitation, she jumped through. She ran without looking.

She ran home. Mother was standing in the kitchen.
'Where's Jane?'
'She came home, but she said she had forgotten something.'
'Well, well, well. When she comes home, I'm going to strangle her!'

Izzy Hamilton (10)
Whitstone Primary School, Devon

THE ANGEL FAMILY

Mel had always been scared of one particular thing, one nobody else knew about. She had always been scared of dying, but now she wondered why all of her friends had always made a big fuss about it. She had died when a friend had said horrible things to her after an argument, which made her leave school early and get knocked down by a confused driver. He didn't think school finishes so early, he had stated.

Mel now felt as free as a bird and could even fly, something she had always wanted to do. She had even tried to thank her friend. She missed chatting to her friends and family and she even missed school sometimes, but not much. She had made new, dead friends and even felt as though she had become part of a new family.

These angels, as she liked to call them had names. Leah, the mum, Jon, the dad, Vicky, the fashion conscious teenager and Ben and Joe, baby twins. It was a very big and loving family to be part of.

Mel counted herself lucky and was a very happy nine-year-old girl from that day onwards.

Stacey Bluett (11)
Whitstone Primary School, Devon

THE SILLY SCIENTIST

It was a cold night, so all the radiators were on. Bob, the scientist, was rummaging around the house, up to his usual tricks, taking light bulbs from lights and taking wires from the radiator sockets. However, Wendy, Bob's wife, was freezing as she lit the fire.

As the sun rose, so did Bob. He got out of bed and went to his lab, leaving Wendy to snore. He set out his tools that he had collected the night before. Carefully he clipped a wire to his nose and the other end to a bulb. That instant, slime appeared in the bulb. He smashed the bulb and swallowed the slime. Suddenly, Bob's whole body began to bulge. Minutes later, Bob was as big as a balloon.

When he returned home, he plodded to the kitchen where his wife, amazingly enough, was reading a science magazine and Bob found himself cooking. He hated cooking. Then Bob felt a twinge and his body shrank to his normal size again.

Ever since then, Wendy has been reading the science magazine and Bob has been doing the cooking. Was it a coincidence, or was some of the green slime still inside him?

Claire Bluett & Samantha Collins (9)
Whitstone Primary School, Devon

THE DISAPPEARANCE

In the year 1827, a farmer who lived in a small cottage on the cliffs of Painswick Valley, was on his way home from visiting his sick mother. It was one-thirty in the morning and the farmer could hardly see the road ahead. He turned to a sharp bend in the road, when he saw a shadowy figure standing in the road. He slammed on the brakes, skidded off the road and hit a tree.

A group of travellers drove past the scene. They claimed they saw a shadowy figure attacking a man in a car that had skidded off the road. The next day, police came to the scene but found no trace that anything had happened, but the farmer's mother had disappeared in the night.

Stephen Martin (10)
Whitstone Primary School, Devon